The Complete Yorkshire Coast and Moors Walker

by Malcolm Boyes
and Hazel Chester

DALESMAN

Publishing Company Ltd

Dalesman Publishing Company

Stable Courtyard, Broughton Hall,
Skipton, North Yorkshire BD23 3AE

First Edition 1995

© Malcolm Boyes and Hazel Chester

Front cover: Robin Hood's Bay from Stoupe Brow
by C. R. Kilvington

A British Library Cataloguing in Publication record
is available for this book

ISBN 185568 085 8

Printed by Hubbards

CONTENTS

INTRODUCTION

This book comprises a selection of walks taken from our popular Dalesman 'Walks from your car' series. Two walks have been taken from our 'Walks in James Herriot Country' book, one from 'Countryside Walks around Scarborough' and three new walks along the coast have also been included.

The 42 walks range from 2.5 to 8.5 miles and cover a vast range of interesting countryside. Along the coast you can walk in the footsteps of smugglers around Flamborough and Hayburn Wyke, visit the scenes of shipwrecks and rescues, go looking for migrating birds at Saltburn or visit the only mainland gannetry at Bempton. Hornsea Mere and Spurn Point further south can provide a wealth of birds at any time of the year.

Inland are the North York Moors offering a mixture of heather moorland that turn into a purple carpet in August and September, riverside walks, ridge walks and wooded valleys covered in deciduous or coniferous trees. Walks visit a number of places of interest which are as varied as the medieval Byland Abbey ruins or the sites of Kirkbymoorside's castles, Nunnington Hall which is in the care of the National Trust, a corpse road between two valleys or a 19th century iron mine in Rosedale.

There is a rich variety of scenery and all the walks are circular. They provide an afternoon walk for a family; take a field guide to flowers and birds and spend some time examining the hedgerows and stream sides, in summer you will be surprised how many different wild flowers you may encounter. With the rich diversity of countryside you will encounter different flowers and birds on different walks. If you become more ambitious a walk can be undertaken in the morning , then after a break at an inn or for a picnic another walk can be undertaken later. On many there are inns on the route or close to the start.

Each walk begins with details of any points of interest on the walk which may be viewpoints, buildings or the scene of a shipwreck giving an indication of what you will find of interest. The walk description begins at the word **START** and a detailed route description follows.

Area covered by this guide

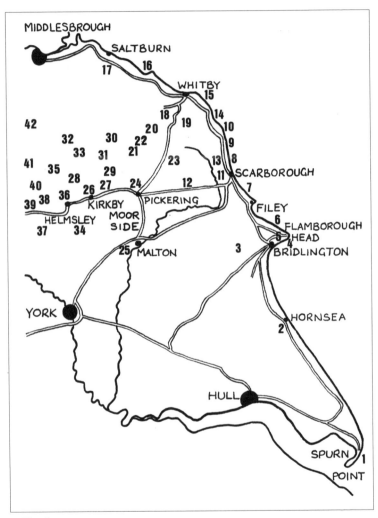

Equipment

On a dry summer afternoon all the walks can be accomplished in sensible walking shoes. After rain or in winter some tracks may become muddy and boots may be preferred. You will require a windproof jacket as moorland breezes can soon make you cold and uncomfortable. With the uncertainties of the weather it is worth taking waterproof clothing. You may wish to take a compass and the relevant Ordnance Survey map, food, a camera, binoculars and field guides to birds and wild flowers. The easiest way to carry everything is in a small rucksack.

Safety
If you have an accident or meet someone else who has had an accident, render what first aid is possible - the local rescue team, or coastguard can be contacted by ringing the police. Don't let members of your group stray out of sight or get left behind. If the moor tops or coast is covered in mist, or likely to become covered in mist, choose a walk in the dale bottoms. The moorland and coastal walks with their extensive views are best walked on clear days. Allow plenty of time to complete your walk before nightfall especially when on the coastal cliff top paths.

Problems with paths
The walk descriptions are correct at the time of writing. Some paths may become overgrown in summer and some may be diverted but the new route will be well signposted. With modern farming methods hedges or stiles may disappear or new buildings may appear around farms, however the path should remain walkable. In case of difficulty contact the Highways Department at County Hall, Northallerton if the problem is in North Yorkshire or County Hall, Beverley if it is Humberside.

Parking
Each of the walks starts from a place where you can park your car, either in a village, in a car park or a piece of land where cars park regularly. Do not obstruct other traffic or farm gateways.

Warning
Thieves operate around some car parks in the area. Do not leave cameras, purses, handbags or other valuables on view in your car. Take them with you or lock them in the boot. Please drive carefully on unfenced moorland roads and give sheep and lambs the right of way.

BRIDLINGTON AND HOLDERNESS

Walk 1   **8.5 miles, 7.5 miles or 1.75 miles**

Spurn Point

Parking: **1.** *For 8.5 mile walk, park in the lane beside the Spurn Heritage Coast* Information Centre (TA 416158)
2. For 7.5 mile walk, use the Canal Scrape car park (TA 416153). 3. For 1.75 mile walk, use the car park at Spurn Head (TA 402110). A fee is payable for access by car to the nature reserve and no dogs are allowed on the reserve.

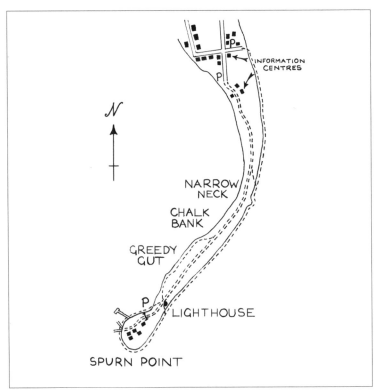

On a fine sunny day Spurn Point can be the most fascinating place in Yorkshire; on a foggy day in winter it can be the most remote and inhospitable place in Yorkshire. Each Spring and Autumn as migrating birds pass along the coast the peninsular can suddenly become alive with birdwatchers as the word goes out that another rare vagrant has been identified. The narrow spit of land is constantly moving westwards as the coast further north erodes away. Winter storms can cause problems as you will see from the road that has been built to reach the people who live on the Point. The peninsular is formed from debris washed down the coast and hopefully there will always be a Spurn Point even though it may have been breached and reformed over the years.

Over 1,000 years ago the Danes landed on Spurn and created a township on the Humber side of the spit of land. It grew into a rich town with two Members of Parliament. Late in the 15th century the town was swept away in storms and the peninsular reformed again. Nothing remains of Ravenser.

The end of the peninsular is inhabited by the crew of the Humber lifeboat, the only full time crew in Britain, and by coastguards monitoring shipping in the Humber Estuary. During the First World War the peninsular was defended by troops against an enemy invasion and a railway line ran from Kilnsea to Spurn Point. Parts of this railway line may be visible as you walk down to the Point. As well as been used by steam engines soldiers used a flat truck with a sail to travel along the railway and an officer took the wheels off his car and converted it to run on the rails.

You have a choice of three starting places for this walk. The longest walk starts at the Information Centre in Kilnsea. The walk can be reduced to 7.5 miles by parking at Canal Scrape car park. The shortest walk is a circuit of the point which will reveal many aspects of Spurn's history and the shipping passing in and out of the River Humber.

START: The Spurn Heritage Coast Project information centre at Kilnsea is housed in the former Blue Bell Inn. The amount of coastal erosion that has occurred in this area over the last 150 years can be seen from two plaques on the building. The original Blue Bell Inn stood in the village of Kilnsea which has disappeared beneath the North Sea. When it was rebuilt on its present site in 1847 the distance to the sea was 534 yards. When the building was restored in 1994 it was 190 yards from the sea. In a little under 150 years the North Sea had moved westwards 344 yards, the fields and buildings had been reduced to debris and washed along the coast, some of which had been deposited along Spurn Point.

At the crossroads beside the information centre turn left towards Spurn Point. Follow the quiet road which leads to the Spurn Point Nature Reserve passing the Canal Scrape car park on the way. At most times of the year you will see birdwatchers scanning the bushes, mudflats and the North Sea for passing birds.

Both the 8.5 mile and 7.5 mile walks continue straight ahead along the road into the nature reserve. Visit the Yorkshire Wildlife Trust information centre which is housed in the first building on your left as you enter. There are a number of books on different aspects of the history and natural history of the area and various pieces of flotsam that have drifted ashore on the Point from various sea creatures. Just beyond the buildings is a Heligoland trap for netting birds. In the last 50 years over 260,000 birds have been ringed to help a world-wide scheme to establish the routes of migrating birds. In 1993 birds ringed at Spurn were discovered in Eire, Spain, Sweden, Germany, Denmark , Norway and Estonia.

Continue along the access road. At Narrow Neck you can follow the old road down the peninsular which was washed away in April 1991. It now leads onto the beach where it originally continued south to the Point. As you continue down the road towards the lighthouse you pass three sections of rail from the former Spurn Point railway set in the road.

Eventually a signposted path on the right takes you away from the access road. This path passes Chalk Bank Hide and later rejoins the road. Near the lighthouse a footpath indicated to Spurn veers of to the right again climbing some steps. This descends to the car park which is the start for the shortest walk of 1.75 miles. If you require refreshments Spurn Bite cafe is straight ahead on your right and is open throughout the year.

To continue all three walks descend onto the beach on the Humber Estuary side of the headland. Walk along the beach passing the jetty used by the Humber Pilots and pass the old lifeboat house. As you walk round the Point you can see Bull Fort out in the Humber Estuary, It was built for defence purposes during the First World War. On the North Sea side of the Point you pass the lofty Coast Guard station controlling passing shipping. Near the lighthouse a path leads back over the sand dunes to the access road where people on the short walk can return to their cars.

For people on the long walks continue back along the beach. About a mile beyond the lighthouse you pass an area near Chalk Bank where the peninsular was cut in 1849. The breach became large enough for the rowing lifeboat to pass through. As you approach the washed away road at Narrow Neck this is where people on the 7.5 mile walk should return to the access road and continue to Canal Scrape car park. People on the 8.5 mile walk can also retrace their steps back to Kilnsea from Narrow Neck or continue along the beach until they meet an exposed pipe extending across the beach. here you can take a ramp up the cliffs to the lane where you parked your car.

Hornsea Mere

Parking: The car park off Newbegin in Hornsea. Set behind Hornsea's Museum (TA 204478).

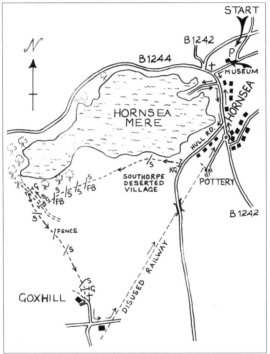

This walk can last for three hours or all day depending on what you want to see. It begins at the North Holderness Museum of Village Life, visits Hornsea Mere which can have a rich variety of birds to see and returns along a former railway line which in summer can be rich in flowers and butterflies. At the end of the walk you pass the entrance to Hornsea Pottery with its many attractions.

The museum in Hornsea is housed in a building which may

date back to the 16th century. For some 300 years it was occupied by members of the Burns Family who carried on a wide range of occupations including weaving, selling sand and gravel that was washed by the sea onto their land, butchers, sexton and coal merchant. The museum contains many items of interest displayed in a natural manner.

Hornsea Mere is the largest fresh water lake in Yorkshire. Its proximity to the sea means it attracts many migrating birds and wildfowl. In winter you may be able to see pochard, shoveler, grebe, divers, goldeneye and pintail. In summer there could be the great crested grebe and little grebe, cormorants or you may be fortunate enough to see a colourful kingfisher diving into the water for a meal. The fields beside the mere may contain greylag and Canada geese .

Hornsea Pottery incorporates a shopping complex as well as a pottery factory shop. There is also an adventure playground and Neptune's Kingdom fantasy world for children. The Yorkshire Car collection, a butterfly world and birds of prey flying displays can prove equally interesting for grown ups.

START: From the car park entrance turn right and walk past the museum. At the traffic lights at the end of the street turn left into Southgate. After 100 yards turn right into the signposted access road to Hornsea Mere if you wish to scan the waters for birds. Return and continue down Southgate. Fork right just before the telephone box along Hull Road and take the footpath on the right. Just beyond the last houses turn right through a large kissing gate signposted 'Public footpath Hornsea Mere'. Bear left across the field following the marker posts, there are excellent views over to Hornsea Mere on the right. The deserted village of Southorpe stood on the slight rise to your left.

At the end of the field cross a stile and the right of way climbs to a post and continues with the hedge on your left but many people seem to follow the foot of the rise. At the end of the field turn right down to the bottom of the slope and turn left through a gateway. Continue on the distinct grass track over the fields keeping straight ahead over three stiles. After crossing a stile and a small footbridge in a hedge bear left across the field to the corner of the wood. Turn right over the stile beside the gate and follow the track to the end of the next field.

At the gate at the end of the field you will see a footpath sign indicating the right of way across the field on your left. Turn back left along this track it goes in a straight line diagonally over the fields to Goxhill. At the end of the first field it crosses a stile to the left of some trees in the hedge. Follow the direction of the waymark arrow as you cross the next field, ignore the metal gate and continue to a wooden fence near the corner of the field where there should be a stile. Continue over the next field to a stile and a grass track leads over the fields towards Goxhill. You join a farm track, after 100 yards when the track bears right carry straight on to a metal gate. Cross the stile in the fence to the left. Cross the field towards the church keeping the pond on your right. Continue through a gate and you reach the road in Goxhill.

Turn left along the quiet road and turn left at the crossroads which is signposted to Hornsea. About 200 yards down the road, just beyond the former Goxhill Station, you turn left at a wooden gate signposted both as a footpath and bridleway. This was the former Hull to Hornsea railway line which opened in 1864 and closed a hundred years later. The sides of the path along the track can be worth exploring for wild flowers in summer. The route passes under the road bridge and continues to a T junction on the outskirts of Hornsea. Turn right and in 20 yards you reach Marlborough Avenue. There is pedestrian access to Hornsea Pottery over to the right. The walk bears round to the left down Marlborough Avenue. At the roundabout take the road signposted to the mere and town centre. Continue back down Southgate to the traffic lights near the church and turn right down Newbegin to the museum and car park.

Rudston, Winifred Holtby Country

Parking: Street parking in Rudston on the B1253 Bridlington to Malton road (TA094678).

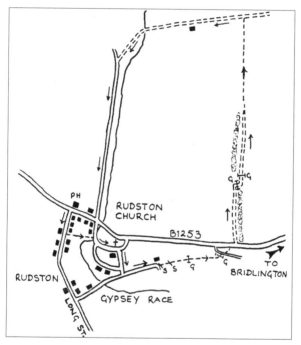

Rudston lies on the rolling countryside of the Yorkshire Wolds some five miles west of Bridlington. The Gypsey Race, one of the few rivers to flow out of the Wolds, passes through the village. On the north side of the churchyard is Rudston Monolith, the largest upright stone in Britain with 25 feet of the stone standing above the ground. For those people with the imagination to appreciate folk lore the story is told of the day that the devil tried to destroy Rudston church. He flung an 80ft spike of rock at the church but missed by a few yards.

Winifred Holtby was born in the village in 1898 and spent her childhood here. She gained a B.A. at Oxford and went on to become a successful novelist and journalist, campaigning vigorously for the rights of women and on behalf of the black people of South Africa. She died at the early age of 37, her most successful book 'South Riding' was published posthumously.

START: Walk down Long Street, the road opposite the Bosville Arms public house. After 100 yards turn left along a tarmac path passing white railings beside the Gypsey Race stream. Turn right at the road, then left around Rose Lodge to pass the south side of the church. Rudston monolith is at the far side of the church. At the lower end of the churchyard, to the left of the tarmac path, is the grave of Winifred Holtby. The gravestone, appropriately, is shaped like an open book. There is another memorial to Winifred Holtby in the church.

From the southern entrance to the church walk down Church Lane which is opposite, the former school is on your right. This hollow way has been in use for centuries as it drops well below the level of the fields. At the T junction turn left along the cul-de-sac road, then keep straight on passing over two stiles with farm buildings on your left. The path continues straight ahead across the fields. It passes through a kissing gate and bears left across the next field to another kissing gate beside a large gate. Cross to the access road and turn right for 20 yards, then turn left to some steps up to the road. Beware of the traffic.

Bear right across the road and turn left along a farm lane with a hedge on your right. At the end of the field follow the lane to the right through a gate, then turn left to another gate. The path continues straight ahead with a hedge on your left, eventually crossing an open field to a farm road. Turn left here for about half a mile to join the road from Rudston to Burton Fleming, it is always worth scanning the hedgerows and fields for birds. Turn left along the road, there is a broad grassy verge on the right and on the left is the deep channel of the Gypsey Race which can often be dry in summer. The stream crosses the Wolds to reach the sea at Bridlington. At the crossroads in Rudston turn right back to the Bosville Arms.

Walk 4   4 mile (5.25 miles including the nature trail.)

Bridlington to Sewerby and Danes Dyke

Parking: Park in Bridlington (TA 193678).

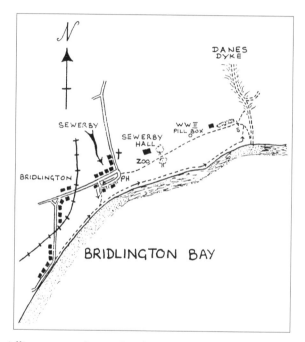

B ridlington nestles under the southern edge of Flamborough Head. This walk follows the cliff top path to Danes Dyke, a part man made and part natural defensive ditch that protected Flamborough in prehistoric times. The return is made passed Sewerby Hall which was built in the 18th century with additions a century later. The hall houses a collection of memorabilia associated with Amy Johnson, the aviator. Also to be seen are paintings, farm implements, a small zoo and a number of sporting opportunities. In Danes Dyke is a nature trail. A small booklet obtained locally describes the Danes Dyke Nature Trail. The trail can be undertaken in conjunction with this walk, but you need the booklet to explain the stops. It passes through a ric-wooded habitat around the former Danes Dyke House and at migration times unusual birds may turn up in the woods. The trail follows the western edge of the valley nearly as far as the Bridlington to Flamborough road, then returns on the eastern side passing the car park and toilets to arrive on the cliff top. There is a series of steps which descend then climb back to rejoin this walk.

START: From the end of North Marine Road in Bridlington, where it leaves the sea front walk straight ahead along a tarmac path. In the summer a 'train' service runs to Sewerby Park from this point. The path soon becomes a cliff top walk with fine views out into Bridlington Bay. The bay is a natural refuge for ships especially in the days of sailing ships. In 1871, 30 ships were sheltering in the bay when they were caught by a south easterly gale which wrecked them against the cliffs.

After three-quarter of a mile you pass the village of Sewerby on your left, then Sewerby Hall set in its own grounds. The cliff top path continues for another mile to reach the top of the steep sided ravine which forms part of Danes Dyke. Turn left along the top of the ravine to a junction of tracks just inside a wood. The path to the right descends steeply to the seashore. Our walk turns left keeping just inside the wood along a stoned path. Just before a stile a path turns right onto the Danes Dyke nature trail at point 4 on the trail.

To return to Bridlington continue over the stile and keep straight ahead with a hedge on your right. Pass some farm build-ings on your right and continue over the fields to a Second World War pill box. The path continues through a small wood and into the grounds of Sewerby Hall. You pass the entrance on your right, then carry straight on between large wire fences forming part of the zoo. This path leads into Sewerby village near the Ship Inn. Walk through the village for 150 yards then turn left at a signpost down a path on to the cliff top. Turn right back into Bridlington the way you came out.

8 miles.

Flamborough: Heroes and Villains

Parking: Street parking in Flamborough village. On the B 1259 Bridlington to Flamborough Head road. (TA 226705).

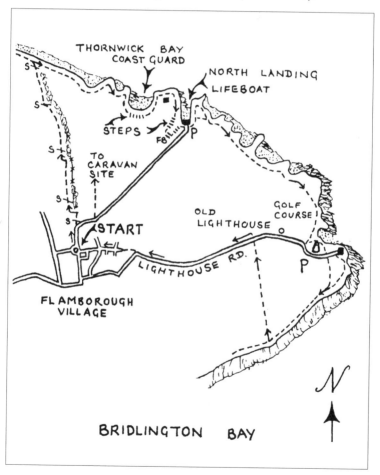

Near the roundabout in the centre of Flamborough village are two memorials to those who lost their lives on this rugged coast. On a calm evening in February 1909 the local fishing cobbles were at sea when a sudden thunderstorm broke; they ran for home as fast as possible. The Gleaner was thrown onto West Scar and the crew John Cross and his sons Robert and Richard Major Cross were thrown overboard. The cobble Two Brothers turned to give assistance, they rescued the men only to have their own boat overturn and all the fishermen lost their lives. The memorial records the names of the crew of the Two Brothers; George Gibbon, Melchior Chadwick and Tom Leng Major.

In 1348 the La Katerine was driven ashore on Flamborough Headland. Thomas Drypool a King's Mariner complained that villains had stolen 200 florins belonging to the king and 100 marks belonging to the mariners as well as goods and timber. The local community also played its part when smuggling was rife in the 18th and 19th centuries. R. D. Blackmore set his smuggling novel Mary Anerley along the coast around Flamborough.

The walk passes a view indicator on Flamborough Head to the Battle of Flamborough Head which took place on the 23 September 1779. John Paul Jones, working for the Americans after their Declaration of Independence, attacked a fleet of 43 ships off the headland. Two English frigates the Serapis and Countess of Scarborough attacked John Paul Jones's ship the Bonhomme Richard. The naval battle was witnessed by crowds of people on the cliff top. The Bonhomme Richard was sunk but not before Jones had captured the Serapis. The 41 merchant ships escaped.

START: Near the roundabout in the centre of Flamborough Village are the two fishermen's memorials. Take the road signposted to North Landing for 350 yards, when the road bears right continue straight ahead to a stile and signposted footpath to North Cliff. At the end of the field the path turns left then right, crossing over a stile. The path now continues with a hedge on the right crossing three stiles to join the coast path after a mile. Turn right along the coast following the cliff top path. There may be a wide variety of birds to be seen in spring and summer from the breeding grounds on the cliffs at Bempton. There is spectacular scenery as the chalk Wolds fall away into the sea. The path skirts Thornwick Bay with its adjacent car park, then steps lead across a ravine and the path passes on the seaward side of some houses. As you approach North Landing there are views of the numerous caves at the foot of the cliffs opposite, including Robin Lyth's Cave named after a notorious smuggler who appears in R. D. Blackmore's Mary Anerley.

On the approach to North Landing, where the lifeboat house is situated on the path again goes inland where steps lead to a footbridge over a ravine. and then continues to the shops and car park. Take the signposted public footpath to the lighthouse, the path keeps to the edge of the fields on your right rather than the cliff top. Eventually the path passes around the golf course to reach the lighthouse on Flamborough Head. On your approach to the lighthouse you pass a replica armada beacon lit to celebrate the 400th anniversary of the defeat of the Spanish Armada in 1988. There is also a view indicator commemorating the Battle of Flamborough Head. Walk around the seaward side of the lighthouse where there are exceptional views into Selwicks Bay. Turn left at the toilets and turn right on the path at the end of the fields.

The path continues on the cliff top walk towards South Landing. After a mile turn right along a signposted path to Lighthouse Road. At the road turn left to Flamborough village. When the road turns left carry straight on over a stile keeping the hedge and fence on your right. The path leads into the village along Stylefield Road. Carry straight on over two road junctions and down Allison Lane. Turn right past the Royal Dog and Duck and left at the Ship Inn into the village centre.

Bempton, Sea Birds and a Lost Village

Parking: The R.S.P.B. car park at the end of Cliff Lane, Bempton, off the B 1229 Scarborough to Flamborough road (TA 197739).

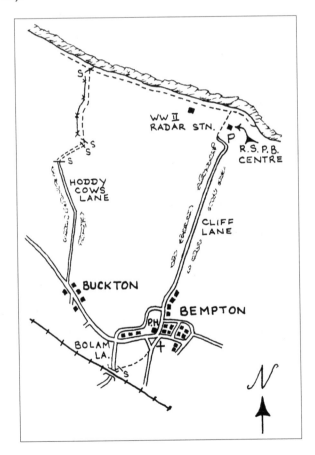

From April to July the 400 foot high sheer cliffs at Bempton become the breeding ground for thousands of sea birds. There are cliff top viewing areas, with a fence to protect you from the sheer drop, where you can look down onto the many birds. They perch precariously on the narrow ledges or can be seen diving into the sea for food for themselves or their young. The most numerous sea bird is the kittiwake but you are also likely to see guillemots, razorbills, herring gulls and the colourful puffin. The walk passes one of the two gannetries on Bempton cliffs and these are the only ones on mainland Britain, the rest being on islands off shore.

In spring and autumn the fields and cliff top hedges can be worth examining for migrating birds. Hoddy Cows Lane may be especially good. The lane may also be worth examining for wild flowers in summer. At Bempton the walk passes close to the site of the former village of Newsham. Around 150 years ago only the house walls remained. It is possible that the inhabitants moved into Bempton. The site of the village has reverted to farmland and is now only remembered from field names.

START: From the large pay and display car park walk over to the RSPB centre where there is information on what birds may be seen in the area. You leave the centre by the opposite door which leads to the path down to the cliffs. If the centre is closed a door to the left should give access to the cliffs. When the path from the RSPB centre reaches the cliffs turn right at the T junction, signposted to Thornwick Bay. After 150 yards stop at the viewpoint with a rail and wire fence, there are views of the sea birds on the cliffs and further afield you can see down to Flamborough Head.

Return to the cliff top path junction and continue straight on to another viewing platform. Continue along the path passing a number of other viewing platforms, around the third and fourth ones you are likely to see the gannets, the adult birds are magnificent white birds with yellow heads and long black tipped wings. On your left across the field are the remains of a Second World War radar station. At the fourth stile turn left along the field signposted to Buckton, keeping the wire fence on your right. There is a tower of a disused windmill on the skyline to act as a guide as you walk to the end of the field. As you approach a broad track turn right over a stile and bear left to another stile on to the track. Turn right along the track passing a pond and gorse bushes, keep your eyes open for birds and wild flowers. Cross the stile beside a gate and continue down Hoddy Cows Lane.

At the road turn left through the village of Buckton and into Bempton. Turn right along Bolam Lane. Before the railway bridge turn hard back left over a stile and cross the field to another stile. The site of the former village of Newsham was just to the south of this path. Continue through a small avenue of trees to two stiles over a ditch, cross the field keeping the hedge and fence on your left. Cross over a stile and bear left around a pond to the church. St Michael's Church is 13th century with a brick chancel added in 1829. Inside there is a fine Early English font. Walk down Church Lane, to the left of the church to reach the White Horse Inn set at the crossroads. Take Cliff Lane, opposite, which leads back to the car park checking the hedgerows for birds as you go.

SCARBOROUGH'S COAST

Walk 7   **3 miles**

Red Cliff Point and Gristhorpe Cliffs

Parking: In the cul de sac road beyond the Plough Inn, Lebberston. (TA 079828). Off the A 165 Scarborough to Bridlington road.

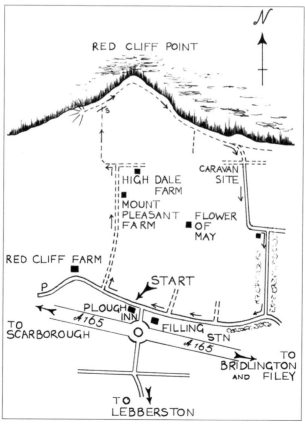

Between Scarborough and Filey the Cleveland Way long distance footpath completes its final section. The fine scenery from the cliff top path is as good as that further north but the area has become extremely popular with caravan owners. This walk out onto the cliff top offers extensive views along the coast and inland to the Yorkshire Wolds. To people staying at the caravan sites it would make an interesting evening stroll in summer with an inn at the finish.

There are excellent views into Cayton Bay to the north where the sailing ship Gainsborough Packet foundered in November 1861. Looking down from Red Cliff Point at low tide you can see the remains of the motor fishing vessel Sincere which was wrecked in thick fog in 1968. There are also extensive views south towards Filey Brigg.

START: Take the minor road passed the Plough Inn and in 300 yards turn right along the signposted public footpath which climbs gently along the access road to Mount Pleasant Farm. If you look back when approaching the farm there are extensive views across the valley to the Wolds and Bempton Cliffs can be seen on the extreme left. When the track turns right carry straight on into the field, there is a yellow waymarker arrow on the wooden post. Turn left and keep the wire fence on your left to the field corner where you turn right. Walk along the edge of the field towards the signpost, cross over the stile onto the cliff top path. Beware of sheer cliffs.

If you walk for about 100 yards to your left, just beyond a wind shaped bush, there is an excellent viewpoint showing the sandy beach at Cayton Bay with the Wolds to the right. Return passed the stile you crossed earlier and descend some steps. Continue on the cliff top path. As you approach Red Cliff Point another view northwards open out on your right showing Scarborough's South Bay with the castle on the headland and Olivers Mount standing out above the town.

Beyond Red Cliff Point another view opens out along the coast south eastwards to Cunstone Nab and Filey Brigg. Down below at low tide you can see the keel and a few remains of a wrecked boat. Continue along the cliff top path, a track to the left near a metal post descends to the stretch of sands below Gristhorpe Cliffs, this is a fairly unfrequented beach. The cliff top path leads eventually to a stile which is a private access path to the Flower of May caravan park, continue, climbing up Mell Casty Hill until you walk along a stoned path with caravans on your right.

At the signpost which indicates the path to Gristhorpe turn right. At the cross roads carry straight on along a tarmac road. There are views of the Wolds ahead. Turn left at the Blue Dolphin reception building and turn right at the next road junction. The access road eventually swings right, parallel with the main road, back to the Plough Inn.

Burniston and Sailor's Grave

Parking: Street parking in Burniston on the A 171 Scarborough to Whitby road or at Crook Ness car park (TA025935).

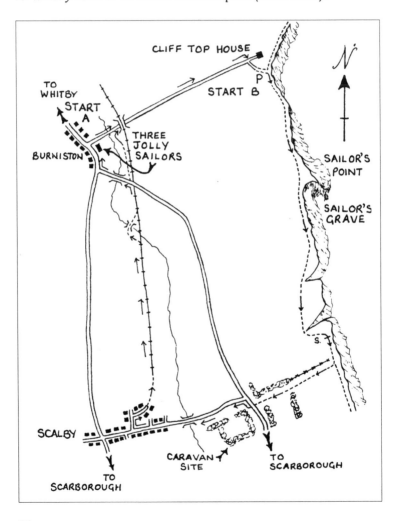

The walk can be started from either Burniston or the small car park on the coast at Crook Ness. The small ravine leading down to the sea may hold sheltering birds during the spring and autumn migration periods, while the surrounding fields and hedges in autumn and winter may reveal, yellowhammers, Lapland bunting, snow bunting or twite. Scanning the sea in winter may reveal divers, grebes or ducks.

Half a mile of cliff top walking with excellent views brings you to Sailor's Grave. Looking down from the cliff top it is hard to imagine a burial taking place on the rocky shore line. Probably it obtained its name from some unfortunate ship being destroyed in a storm. In the 19th century at least three sailing ships were stranded along this stretch of coast, the New Unity in 1869, the William and Ann in 1878 and the William and George which foundered in 1894. During the First World War the danger to shipping increased with mines and U Boats. In 1918 the Madame Renee was sunk by U Boat 30 just off shore but three days later the same U Boat was sunk off Whitby with depth charges.

The return to Burniston is made along the former Scarborough to Whitby railway line. This scenic line offered excellent views of both the sea and the moors. It was opened in July 1885 and closed in March 1965. There were railway stations at Scalby and Cloughton but not at Burniston. The rail fare from Scalby to Scarborough in the 1880s was 5d (2p) for first class passengers and 2.5d (1p) for third class passengers.

START: Walk down Rocks Lane which is to the left of the 'Three Jolly Sailors' inn. Pass under a disused railway bridge and continue along the road. After three-quarter of a mile turn right near the entrance to Cliff Top House and follow the road to the small car park at Crook Ness.

From the small car park at Crook Ness follow the path to the coast which descends a small ravine and turn right, cross over the stream and climb a flight of steps. Continue along the cliff top path which is part of the Cleveland Way long distance footpath. There are good marine views from the top of the 150 foot high cliffs.

Beyond the first headland look back and down to the sea shore where there are some unusual rock formations forming a small natural harbour. This area is Sailor's Grave. Continuing on the cliff top path you can see Scarborough Castle on its headland to the south. A mile and a quarter south of Crook Ness you pass a ravine that cuts inland, a short while later cross over a stile and in about 100 yards turn right through a gateway with an upright post on the right. Walk alongside the wire fence crossing two fields to reach a stile which gives access to the main coast road. Turn right alongside the road and in fifty yards turn left along the road signposted to Scalby Village.

After half a mile take the third road on the right, Field Close Road, there is a sign 'Railway route first right' on the fence on the right. Turn right down Lancaster Way and turn right immediately before the last house. Follow the path around the house to a stile which gives access to the disused railway track. Continue back towards Burniston, crossing the stream on a footbridge to the left of the track. On reaching the road turn left back into Burniston.

For walkers with cars at Crook Ness car park continue along the railway line, on the left at the other side of the road. When you reach the bridge over the road turn left and descend some steps, turn right under the bridge and continue along the road turning right to the car park.

Hayburn Wyke,
a smugglers cove

Parking: Street parking in Cloughton on the A 171 Scarborough to Whitby road or at the small car park at Cloughton Wyke reached along a gated road (TA 018951).

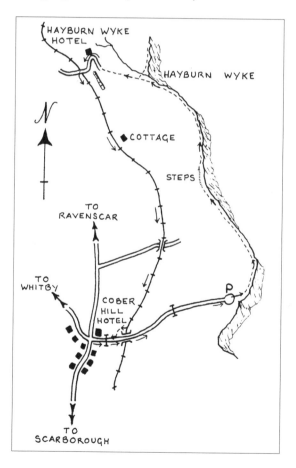

S muggling reached its peak in the 18th century, declining after the Napoleonic Wars. Any goods which were highly taxed in Britain could be smuggled in from the continent showing a huge profit for the people involved in the trade. The smuggling trade involved all classes of society from the sailors who brought the goods to the shore line, the labourer who carried the goods to safe storage places, the people with carts and pannier ponies who transported the goods, the tradesman who sold on the smuggled goods and the rich families who financed the deals.

In Britain in the 1780s a gallon of brandy cost 5s 6d (27.5p), after paying all the people involved in the trade smuggled brandy was being sold at 3s-3d (16p) a gallon. A wide range of goods were smuggled into the country besides spirits. There was tea, cloth and silk, chocolate, playing cards, spinning wheels, pepper and snuff.

Quiet coves like Hayburn Wyke with a route inland through uninhabited countryside would make an ideal landing place. Other goods were brought into harbours concealed in the holds to be removed when the time was right.

The cliff top walk to Hayburn Wyke is along the Cleveland Way. The 112 mile long walking route begins in Helmsley and crosses the Hambleton and Cleveland Hills to reach the coast at Saltburn. The walk then follows the cliffs south through Whitby and Scarborough to join the Wolds Way long distance footpath at Filey Brigg. The return is made along the former Scarborough to Whitby railway line which was opened in July 1885 and closed in March 1965. The sides of the railway are well wooded and may be worth examining for woodland birds.

START: At the road junction at the northern end of Cloughton, where the road curves left to Whitby and straight on for Ravenscar, turn right down the road at the side of the 'Cober Hill Hotel'. After 100 yards carry straight on through a gate and follow the road across the field and over a bridge across the disused railway. After passing through another gate you reach a small car park.

At the far end of the car park a path leads down some steps

towards the sea. Bear left onto the cliff top path which is part of the Cleveland Way long distance footpath. There are many excellent views as you walk north up the coast. After 300 yards cross a small stream and later climb 67 steps up a hillside. The cliff top path continues along the edge of the fields offering occasional glimpses into the remote undercliff above the sea shore. Eventually the path crosses a stile and descends through a wood. Turn left at a signpost indicating the Cleveland Way. After ten yards cross a stile and walk over a field to a stone wall and turn right up a track which leads to the Hayburn Wyke Hotel.

The hotel is set in a remote valley and a path leads down to the sea shore where a small waterfall drops onto the beach. Turn sharp left as you approach the hotel along the access road. When you cross the former railway line turn left through a gate onto the former railway track. Walk along the track for 1.5 miles until a bridge passes over the top. Turn right up a set of steps and cross a stile onto a road. Turn right back along the road into Cloughton or left to the car park at Cloughton Wyke.

The Three Lords Stone, Ravenscar

Parking: Station Square, Ravenscar, (NZ 984013). Ten miles north of Scarborough.

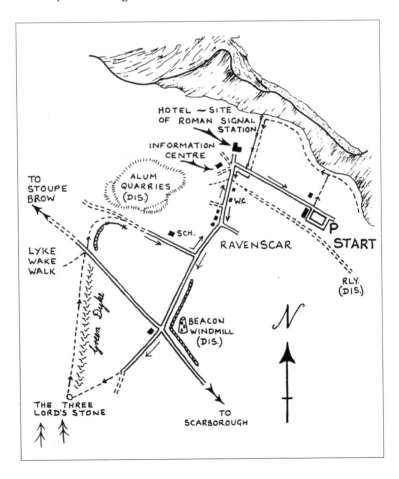

The walk starts out along the cliff top path passing the site of two shipwrecks. One morning in January 1913 the villagers awoke to find the 3,290 ton steamship Coronation fast on the rocks. The ship was returning from Bremen to Sunderland in ballast when she ran into a south easterly gale and a snowstorm. She ran aground at the foot of the 600 foot high cliffs at about 3.25 in the morning. The distress signals from the ship went unnoticed so a crew of volunteers took a line ashore and rigged a bosun's chair to take the rest of the crew off the ship. After various salvage attempts the ship was refloated in September and taken to Hartlepool. A month later the wreck caught fire and was burnt out.

Nearly 52 years later the 1,542 ton motor vessel Fred Everard ran ashore in a snowstorm at the same place. The crew of 14 were rescued by Whitby lifeboat and the ship soon became a total wreck. Some of the wreckage may be visible at low tide.

The walk crosses over the Scarborough to Whitby railway line but the line was taken through a tunnel at this point so as not to disturb W. H. Hammond the owner of the Raven Hall Hotel. The walk then heads out of Ravenscar to the Three Lords Stone. Actually two of the Lords stone survive marking where their boundaries met one is marked with a C+, the other with a SD in a flowing style. They marked the limits the Cholmley's estate who took over Whitby Abbey's land after the dissolution of the monastery, the Hoby estate based at Hackness and the Lordship of Staintondale.

START: Station Square is reached by turning right near the Raven Hall Hotel. It takes its name from the railway station that stood on the western side of the square. Walk eastwards down to the cliff top path and turn left. The views are spectacular and you can see why the shipwreck of the Coronation went unnoticed. When the cliff top path reaches a fence turn left up the broad track to the road. Turn right, then left on the road that leads out of Ravenscar. There are extensive views on your right down into Robin Hood's Bay and the township of Robin Hood's Bay can be seen set in and above the ravine. There is a broad grassy strip beside the road as you walk out of Ravenscar. When the road to Scarborough turns sharp left, near the old windmill, carry straight on along a broad track. There is an extensive view southwards to Filey Brigg, Bempton Cliffs and Flamborough Head.

When the track turns left pass over a stile straight in front of you. Follow the path across the moor to the wood corner. Cross the wire fence by a stile and your track turns right beside the fence. First take a look to the left of the stile, near the wood, where you will find the two inscribed stones marking their lordship's boundary. The path to the right of the stile follows Green Dike towards the radio mast on the skyline. This distinct earthwork may date back to prehistoric times It also forms the boundary of Staintondale township and the boundary between the wapentakes of Pickering Lythe and Whitby Strand.

When you reach the road there is a stone indicating the end of the 40 mile Lyke Wake Walk which crosses the moors from Osmotherley. Cross the road and follow the signposted footpath with a ditch and stone wall on your right. As you walk down the track extensive views over Robin Hood's Bay open up. The path turns right following a wire fence and eventually becomes a road. Turn left at the junction back into Ravenscar. Turn right at the Raven Hall Hotel entrance back to Station Square.

SCARBOROUGH'S COUNTRYSIDE

Walk 11   **4.25 miles**

Forge Valley

Parking: Either street parking in West Ayton on the A170 Scarborough to Pickering road or there are two car parks at the top end of Forge Valley at (SE 983876).

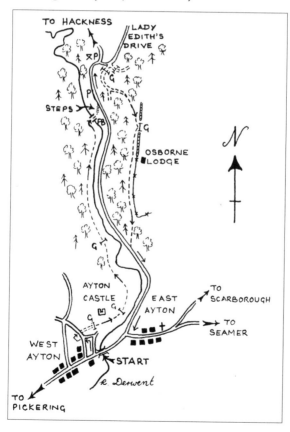

The River Derwent has cut out this steep sided valley on its way inland to join the River Ouse. The greater part of the valley is covered in trees, oak on the upper slopes with ash, elm, alder and willow lower down the slopes. The area forms a National Nature Reserve and among the birds to be seen are nuthatch, a variety of tits, chiff chaff, greater spotted woodpecker chaffinch and jay as well as grey squirrels. There is a picnic site and car park halfway round the walk, if you park your car here begin reading the walk at paragraph three.

START: From the bridge between East and West Ayton, looking upstream, take the road on your left, Mill Lane, and at the fork turn left to join Yedmandale Road. Turn right up the road and turn right again along Castle Rise. At the end of the row of houses pass through a wicket gate and walk past the ruins of Ayton Castle on your left. The castle was once owned by the Eure family.

Continue on the track and turn left at the signpost at the start of the next field. Skirt the edge of the field eventually joining a riverside path into Forge Valley. Continue alongside the stream for a mile crossing over the river at the Jubilee Footbridge erected by Scarborough Scout Association in 1977. Take the path straight ahead which climbs some steps and bears left to the road. Beware of traffic as you walk up to the car park which is also a bird feeding station. Ten minutes watching the birds here should give the opportunity to see seven or eight species. Continue along the road to a road junction where there is a picnic site on your left. This is the alternative start to the walk.

Walk straight ahead along Lady Edith's Drive and after seventy yards turn sharp back right through a gate. Follow the broad track uphill, fork left after half a mile and the path climbs steeply through the wood to a gate into a field. Do not pass through the gate but turn right inside the edge of the wood, the path passes Osborne Lodge on your left. After half a mile the path descends to a road, turn left along the footpath which climbs then descends into East Ayton. Ayton Castle can be seen again at the top of the hill on your right. Turn right at the main road back to the bridge over the River Derwent.

Brompton and Sawdon

Parking: Brompton on the A 170 Scarborough to Pickering road, park in the side streets off the main road (SE 943821).

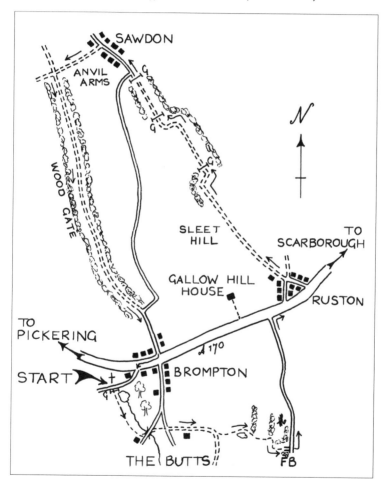

Brompton has some delightful areas which are missed by the motorist speeding along the main road. Just below the church the walk passes a pond which drains onto The Butts. You may see mute swans, moorhen, coot, little grebe, tufted duck and mallard while in winter there may also be pochard, goldeneye and teal. The paths on this walk are bordered by good thick hedgerows and you may see a variety of song birds.

This village is where aviation first began when a heavier-than-air machine carried Sir George Cayley's coachman across Brompton Dale in 1853. Sir George Cayley, the local squire, designed the first aeroplane with moveable tailplane to steer and wheeled undercarriage but there was no engine available to carry his ideas any further. That would not happen until we entered the 20th century.

Brompton church was the scene of the marriage of William Wordsworth to Mary Hutchinson in 1802. The couple had met when they were at school in Penrith. The walk passes around the land of Gallows Hill Farm where Mary Hutchinson's family lived. The place is now open to the public and there is an exhibition on Wordsworth and Coleridge, an art gallery, woodland walk, tea rooms and gift shop.

START: From the church entrance in Church Lane pass through the gate opposite and follow the edge of the field, with the stream and pond on your left. As you approach the building at the end of the field the stream drops over a weir. Pass through a gate, to the left of the building and descend some steps continuing to the road. Turn left and pass over a small bridge on the spacious green. Continue on the side road across The Butts. At the road junction carry straight on across the green heading for the left hand side of some white railings. Cross over the road and walk down the lane opposite.

The lane passes straight through a farmyard and continues along the edge of the fields; eventually when the lane turns right carry straight on with a hedge on your right. Skirt a small pond and cross a ditch at the end of the field by a small wooden bridge. At the end of the next field bear right and continue with the hedge on your left to reach the road by crossing a small footbridge. Turn left along the country road. Gallows Hill House, the home of Mary Hutchinson's family can be seen slightly to the left. If you wish to visit the place turn left at the main road and turn right up the access road.

To continue the walk cross the main road and turn right, bearing left into the village of Ruston. Continue bearing left at the road junction in the village passing a Victorian letter box set in the wall. The road changes to a lane which rises gently; eventually it turns right then left through a white gate. At the end of the field follow the track which turns left then right and continues straight ahead through a gate into Sawdon. Walk straight ahead through the village. The Anvil Arms Inn on your left was originally the blacksmith's shop and the forge can still be seen in the bar.

On the outskirts of the village turn left along a tarmac road past Hallykeld House. After 200 yards turn left at the crossroads down a broad lane. There are widespread views over the Vale of Pickering to the Wolds beyond. After a mile the lane merges with the road to Brompton. Continue down the road. Turn right along the main road and turn left just beyond the Cayley Arms back into Brompton.

Scalby Sea Cut

Parking: Street parking in Scalby, Two miles north of Scarborough. (TA 009902). Off the A 171 Scarborough to Whitby road.

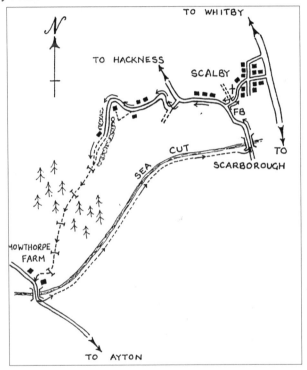

The Scalby Sea Cut was dug by hand in the first decade of the 19th century. It was the idea of Sir George Cayley, the squire at Brompton (see Walk 12) to prevent seasonal flooding in the area between Scarborough and Pickering. The intention was to divert the River Derwent's floodwater along the Sea Cut and into the North Sea enabling an improvement in farmland alongside the river in the Vale of Pickering. In late summer there may be only 3m gallons of water a day flowing along the Sea Cut but this can build up to 540m gallons a day after storms. The River Derwent begins its journey about six miles from the sea but after crossing 50 miles of countryside it enters the River Ouse further from the sea than when it started — the river flows inland.

The walk begins from Scalby church. Parts of the church date back to the 12th century and during the intervening years it has had at least two noted vicars. William Mompesson was the vicar at Scalby before moving to Eyam in Derbyshire. In 1665-6 the plague struck Eyam and William Mompesson persuade the villagers to isolate themselves from the surrounding villages to stop the plague spreading. Between September 1665 and October 1666 259 villagers died out of a population of 350 but the disease did not spread. Another vicar was the brother of Adam Sedgwick, the noted Yorkshire geologist.

START: From the entrance to St. Laurence's church in Scalby walk down the road away from the Nags Head Hotel. The road swings right around the churchyard. Cross the bridge over the stream and at the crossroads turn right up Hay Lane. After quarter of a mile turn left, near the National Park boundary sign, along the footpath to Scalby Nabs. Follow the road around the bends, climb past East Farm and Keld Runnels Farm. There are good views to your left over Scalby Sea Cut which you will use for your return.

The access road becomes an unsurfaced lane called Keld Runnels Road and continues for a mile. Pass through a gate and bear right in 50 yards through the gateway on the right. Follow the bottom edge of the field keeping the wire fence on your left. Carry straight on at the next gateway climbing slightly to a gate which leads to a path through the wood. Pass through another gate at the end of the wood and continue along the edge of the field keeping the wire fence on your left. Pass through the next gate and a track descends along a sunken lane to reach a gate near a farm. After passing through the gate turn right, then left, between the farm buildings to reach the road at Mowthorpe

Farm. Beware of traffic as you turn left along the road. Cross over the bridge and turn left over a stile. You are now faced with a pleasant walk back to Scalby along the bank of the Sea Cut. There are open views to the right across the fields to the wooded hillside covered by Raincliffe Woods. East Ayton Moor above the woods was the site of Seamer Beacon when the threat of a Napoleonic Invasion existed. When you reach the road in Scalby turn left over the bridge across the Sea Cut and continue down the road. After about 400 yards turn right over a white footbridge and right again back up the road to Scalby church.

WHITBY'S COAST

Walk 14

4 miles

Robin Hood's Bay
and Boggle Hole

Parking: The large car park in Robin Hood's Bay (NZ 950054). South of Whitby.

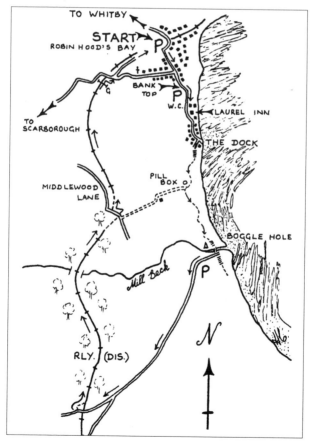

A picturesque fishing village, a cliff top walk and a return journey along a disused railway combine to make an interesting walk. The narrow pathways through Robin Hood's Bay town tempt people to explore the village further. The quaintly named Boggle Hole takes its name from a local folklore ghost who probably inhabited the small valley. The return journey along the former railway track is through well wooded terrain and offers the possibility of seeing a variety of woodland birds.

As you walk through Bay Town, as Robin Hood's Bay is known locally, you can soon get the feel of this place which earned its living from fishing — but many years ago smuggling was also just as profitable and widespread. Ulric Walmsley moved to the town with his wife and small child in 1894. He was a painter and his young son Leo went to the local school and learnt how to handle boats and fishing nets. These experiences he recalled in his books, the best known being Three Fevers which was turned into the film Turn of the Tide many years ago. His fictitious name for Bay Town was Bramblewick.

START: From the car park entrance on the Whitby road turn right down the hill to Bank Top. On the right near the toilets is a plaque recording the rescue of the crew of the Visitor which sank in the bay in 1881. The lifeboat had to be brought overland from Whitby through snow drifts. Descend the steep bank into the old fishing village — you may find the steps on the left more convenient. Access to the village is restricted for motor vehicles. The road turns left and then right near the Laurel Inn, the villagers had great difficulty manoeuvring the rowing lifeboat around this corner to rescue the crew of the Visitor.

Cross over the small bridge and follow the road down to The Dock where there is access to the beach. To the left of the slipway is the Bay Hotel, which has the distinction of having a ship-wrecked against its walls during a storm in 1893. Turn back into the town and in 50 yards turn left along Albion Street, this is also the route of the Cleveland Way long distance footpath. At the end of the short street turn left up a series of steps, this leads to a board walk which bears right up to the cliff top path. Continue walking along the path which offers splendid views over the bay to Ravenscar. Eventually the path descends to Boggle Hole youth hostel. Originally this was the corn mill for the people of Robin Hood's Bay and was destroyed in a flood in 1857.

Cross the footbridge and follow the path to the road where you turn right. Pass the roadside car park and continue along the road for three-quarter of a mile. There are good views on the left towards Ravenscar. Fork right at the road junction along the road signposted to Fylingthorpe. Cross over a stream in the wood and shortly turn back right onto the railway track bed.

The line was opened in 1885 and closed under the Beeching Plan in 1965. It provided some spectacular sea views on its journey from Whitby to Scarborough. The track bed offers easy walking with no route finding difficulties. There is a slight deviation to cross Middlewood Lane and then the track continues into the outskirts of Robin Hood's Bay. When you reach the road turn right for 40 yards, then turn left up the road signposted 'village hall'. This leads back into the car park.

Historic Whitby

Parking: *There is a large car park near the railway station and also street parking in the town (NZ 899111).*

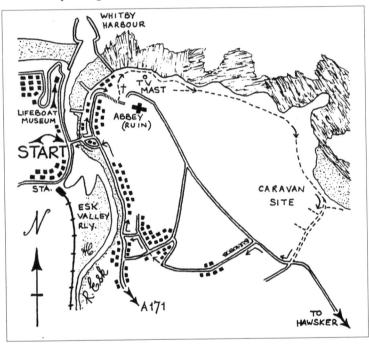

Whitby has a rich heritage of interesting buildings and places associated with well known people. The walk begins by crossing the bridge between the two sides of the town standing on either bank of the River Esk. The bridge swings on its central axis to allow boats to pass through and enter the inner harbour. The quaint cramped houses that cling to the riverbank on either side of Church Street lead up to the foot of the 199 Steps.

As you approach the top of the steps you pass the Caedmon Memorial which was unveiled by Alfred Austin, the poet laureate in September 1898. The carved sandstone cross commemorates Caedmon a lay brother at nearby Whitby Abbey in the 7th century. He was a simple local peasant with no talent for singing or composing music but after a dream in which he sang religious verses he went on to compose a large amount of Saxon verse and attempted to produce a vernacular version of the bible. He became a monk at Whitby Abbey and is now accepted as the father of English sacred music.

At the top of the 199 Steps is St Mary's Church a quaint and fascinating building with box pews, many marked with the names of surrounding villages for which they were reserved. The whole interior of the church with its upper gallery is quaint and unusual, it was fitted out by Whitby shipwrights in 1612. There is an ear trumpet beside the pulpit to enable the deaf wife of the vicar to hear his sermons. On the outside of the building tucked away under a staircase is a memorial to Francis and Mary Huntrodds, they were both born on the same day, married on that same date of the year and both died within five hours on that same date 80 years later. Close by is Whitby Abbey now in the care of English Heritage with an interesting display showing its history from the time of Saint Hilda in the 7th century.

The cliff top walk passes the scene of the Rohilla shipwreck in 1914. The story of the many hours of rescue attempts to save the crew and personnel on the hospital ship is told in Whitby's Lifeboat Museum. The walk returns to the banks of the river Esk at the site of the Horngarth ceremony where each year on the eve of Ascension Day a woven wooden hedge is planted in the harbour at low tide. It is a penance for the killing of a hermit in medieval times. The final place of interest on the walk is the Captain Cook Memorial Museum in Grape Lane where the famous navigator lodged with his employer while he learned his apprenticeship as a seaman.

START: Cross the swing bridge over the River Esk into old Whitby nestling below the abbey. Take the second turn left along cobbled Church Street, keep your eyes open for the quaintly named Arguments Yard on your left. The road bears right around W Hammond's jet manufacturer's shop — this was an industry that boomed in Whitby in Victorian times. Begin climbing the 199 Steps — you can always pause and look back across the harbour to the West Cliff with is whalebone arch and statue of Captain Cook. As you approach the top of the flight of steps you pass Caedmon's Cross on your left. To reach the entrance to Whitby Abbey continue straight ahead through the churchyard to reach the car park at Abbey Plain and turn right.

The walk turns left along the path nearest the cliff which passes to the left of St Mary's church. Continue along the cliff top bearing right to the TV mast and take the path to the left. There are excellent coastal views from the cliff top path. After half a mile you pass Saltwick Nab the scene of the Rohilla shipwreck. Details and memorabilia of the disaster can be seen in Whitby's Lifeboat Museum. The path leads through Saltwick Bay caravan site, follow the signs through the site and pass through the entrance. You now leave the coast and follow the access road down to the main road to Whitby Abbey.

Turn right along the road and at the end of the field on your left turn left between a hedge and a wire fence. The path leads down to a group of buildings, walk on between the buildings. After a further 300 yards the access road swings right, continue straight ahead along a flagged path which leads to a road. Take the street opposite 'The Ropery' and turn left beyond the telephone box.

Descend 'Salt Pan Well Steps' then cross over the road to the side of the River Esk. Turn right and in 50 yards you reach the plaque marking the site of the Horngarth or Penny Hedge ceremony. Continue walking into Whitby and turn left along Grape Lane. Pass the Captain Cook Memorial Museum where James Cook lodged with his shipowner master. Turn left at the end of the lane to cross back over the swing bridge. To visit the Lifeboat Museum turn right along the riverside for about 200 yards, it is on your left just before the Khyber Pass.

Runswick and Port Mulgrave

Parking: The cliff top car park, Runswick (NZ 807161). Off the A 174 Whitby to Saltburn road.

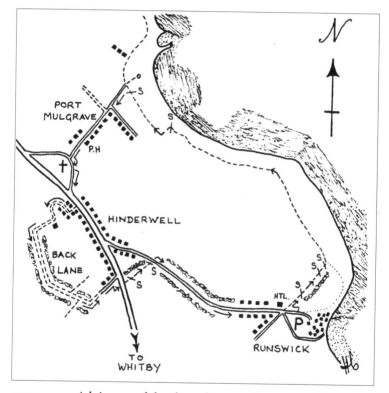

Runswick is one of the three famous picturesque fishing villages on the Yorkshire Coast. Both Staithes and Robin Hood's Bay have narrow alleyways running between the cramped houses. Runswick is more spacious which allows the added charm of colourful gardens and open views from the village into Runswick Bay.

Across Runswick Bay from the village lies the headland of Kettleness which was the scene of a number of shipwrecks which kept the local lifeboat crew busy. If a ship became stranded on the rocks the local fishermen were always willing to lighten the cargo to assist with floating the ship off the rocks at high tide. The payment for their work was with the offloaded coal being placed in their boats and rowed ashore. From 1911 one local man managed to accumulate enough coal from wrecks to save him buying any for 20 years.

The village and its lifeboat achieved national fame in 1901 when the women of the village launched the rowing lifeboat. The fishing cobbles had all left at dawn to go fishing, during the morning a wind blew up eventually increasing to gale force. The cobbles could be seen by the villagers being tossed around on the horizon and there was no one to launch or man the lifeboat. A scratch crew of older fishermen and farm workers were gathered and the women of the village dragged the heavy rowing lifeboat across the beach and pushed it until they were waist deep in the water to float the boat off its cradle. The lifeboat then escorted the cobbles back to the beach with no loss of life. The women of the village were later given a celebration dinner in Manchester to mark their service and achievement.

START: From the top car park at Runswick turn left and walk along the road to the Runswick Bay Hotel. Turn right at the Cleveland Way sign, not along Lingrow Close. Pass through the hotel car park and cross over three stiles to reach the cliff top path. Turn left along the cliff top where there are spectacular views along the coast. After a quarter of a mile you pass the site of a failed mining venture. An iron mine, kilns and furnaces were built on a shelf of rock near the bottom of the cliffs. In 1858 after the plant had produced only 100 tons of iron there was a landslip and the site had to be abandoned.

Steps descend in and out of a small valley and after a mile the path turns sharp left, it then follows the edge of the fields round to Port Mulgrave. At this point there are excellent views down to the former harbour which is now being destroyed by the sea.

It was built to transport iron ore and the ore arrived on the quay through a railway tunnel from the mines inland. When you reach the road turn right to an information board about Port Mulgrave. A path leads steeply down to the harbour and it is a steep ascent back up but if you have time it is worth the effort.

Return and walk along the road through Port Mulgrave, there is an inn in the village. The terraces of houses were built for workers at the ironstone mines. Continue along the road to the junction with Hinderwell Church in front of you. Turn left, then right up the steps into the churchyard. St Hilda's Well from which the village takes its name, is set behind the church down some steps. It is dedicated to St Hilda who founded Whitby Abbey in 657.

Return through the same churchyard gate and continue down the footpath into Hinderwell. At the junction cross over the road and walk down West End Close, opposite. Turn right along Porret Lane which swings left, then turns right and left along Back Lane. Turn left at the end of the lane into the outskirts of Hinderwell. Turn right at the main road as far as the speed limit sign. Turn left along the signposted public footpath to a stile, continue with the hedge on your left to another stile onto a road. Turn right along the roadside path to Runswick. At the road junction in Runswick take Bank Top Lane opposite that leads back to the car park. If you are not too tired continue along the lane which descends turning right to the outskirts of Runswick village. Turn left along the first stepped path into the village and meander your way through the paths exploring all the nooks and corners of this charming village. Return back to the car park by the same route as you descended.

Saltburn Gill and
the Heritage Coast

*Parking: Old Saltburn car park (NZ 668215). Alternatively
park in Saltburn and walk down the hill to Old Saltburn.*

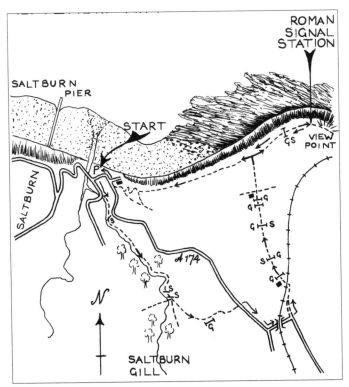

Saltburn stands on the cliff top overlooking Old Saltburn
which was the original fishing village. Saltburn was built in
the second half of the nineteenth century after the railway
line had been built from Redcar in 1861. Old Saltburn was just

an inn and a few houses nestling under Huntcliff. Earlier in the century the hamlet was known as a smuggling centre. The most famous smuggler was John Andrews who ran the Ship Inn. There is now a Smugglers Heritage Centre near the inn which is open to the public.

The walk leaves the coast up Saltburn Gill, a nature reserve. On a summer afternoon we saw and heard goldfinch, chaffinch, yellowhammer, house sparrow, wren and pied wagtail. Early in a morning or at migration times in May, September and October a far richer variety of birds might be discovered. The walk climbs out of the valley and up to Brotton. The walk across the fields to the cliff top path reveals extensive views over Saltburn to the industrial complex around Teesside.

A walk along the cliff top path leads to the sight of a Roman signal station. It was one of a series built along the coast to warn of raiders from the sea. There are extensive views taking in many miles of the Durham coast to the north of the Tees Estuary. The return to Old Saltburn is along the Cleveland Way long distance footpath. Walkers on this trail will have walked sixty miles over the moors from Helmsley to Saltburn where they begin the 52 mile cliff top walk to Filey Brigg.

START: From the car park entrance, near the toilets, turn right away from the sea. Cross the road bridge over the stream and turn left at the foot of the hill along the signposted public foot-path. Cross over to the footbridge and turn right on the far bank of Saltburn Gill. Eventually a stile leads into Saltburn Gill Nature Reserve. Keep to the distinct path through the valley and observe the rules. After half a mile you will see a footbridge over Saltburn Gill, after crossing two stiles turn immediately left on the path that climbs out of the valley — keep a wooden fence on your left.

At the top of the valley side the path turns right to a field. Fork left along the side of the field with a wooded valley to your left. Just before you reach a gate fork left on a path and keep a wood-en fence on your left to reach a tarmac access road. Turn right and follow the drive to the main road. Turn right on the foot-path into Brotton. Take care when the footpath ends and pass under the railway bridge. When the main road turns sharp right turn left along the access road.

Walk down the lane and cross over the railway to reach Shepherd's House. Bear left in the farmyard to a gate and follow the track over the fields to Brough House Farm. There are excellent views to the left over Saltburn to Teesside. Pass through the farmyard to a signpost where tracks cross and take the broad track straight ahead signposted 'cliff path'.

When you reach the cliff top turn right. The path climbs gently for 500 yards, about 100 yards beyond the gate you reach the Roman signal station which is marked by an information plaque. A further hundred yards along the cliff top path there is a view south-eastwards along the coast to Boulby Cliffs, the highest point on the east coast of England.

Return back along the cliff top path to where you joined it and continue straight ahead descending towards Old Saltburn. It may be worth watching the skies and sea for gulls and cormorants. Set above the hamlet is a stone carved with the words 'Cleveland Heritage Coast' and ammonite fossils. Steps descend to the road where you turn right passed the Ship Inn. Continue along the coast until you see the car park on your left from where you started.

Featherbed Lane

Parking: The car park to the south of the road bridge in Sleights (NZ 867080). on the A 169 Whitby to Pickering road.

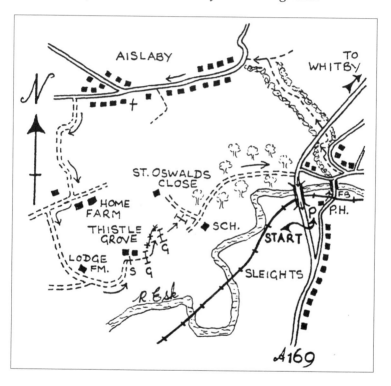

S leights lies in the Esk Valley on the busy main road from Pickering to Whitby. This delightful walk uses what has been termed the narrowest highway in England. Featherbed Lane is a flagged pathway which is just wide enough for pedestrians and packhorses with their panniers. The walk uses the path to climb from Sleights in the valley to Aislaby on the edge of the moors where there are excellent views. The walk passes two inns, it is easy for route finding and makes a good introduction for novice walkers. The return is made past crenellated St Oswald's Close and through deciduous woodland.

START: From the car park entrance turn left past the Salmon Leap Hotel and descend to the railway station. Cross over the railway line and the footbridge into Briggswath, the small community gathered on the northern bank of the River Esk. Turn right for 25 yards, then turn left across the road and up a narrow paved path indicated by a sign 'Featherbed Lane', ignoring the steps on the right. Follow the flagged path which climbs steadily towards Aislaby crossing the Whitby to Pickering road on the way.

Near the top the path turns left to enter Aislaby. Carry straight on along the road through the village passing The Huntsman Inn on your right. Fork left along the road past the church. After 300 yards turn left at a public bridleway sign and follow the farm road. Turn right past Coachman's Cottage and turn left to Lodge Farm.

At Thistle Grove turn right over a stile signposted 'Sleights bridleway'. Follow the ancient paved path which passes below the crenellated St Oswald's Close, this leads to a gate onto an access road. Turn right, downhill, for 20 yards, then turn left along the access road. Pass through deciduous woodland to reach the main road. Cross over the road and turn right over the bridge. There is a plaque commemorating the bridge's reconstruction after the original bridge had been washed away in a flood in 1930. At the far side of the bridge turn left back to the car park.

Falling Foss and Littlebeck

Parking: Falling Foss car park (NZ 888035). Signposted from Red Gates on the B1416 three miles south of Ruswarp.

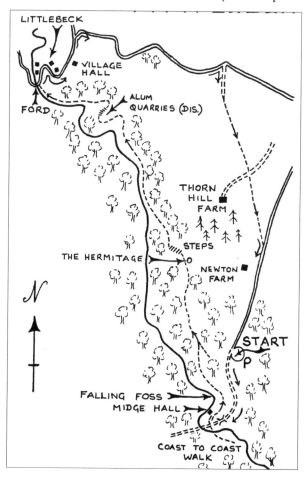

This splendid woodland walk gives an opportunity to see and identify a number of wild flowers in summer and woodland birds. Falling Foss waterfall tumbles 67 feet over a rocky cliff and the walk later passes The Hermitage a rock shelter carved from a single boulder from which there are excellent woodland views. Approaching the pretty hamlet of Littlebeck you pass some alum quarries. This valuable chemical was used for fixing colours when dyeing cloth and in paper and leather manufacturing. The shale was quarried out of the hillside and piled into massive heaps which were set alight. The resulting burnt shale was placed in leaching tanks and was later processed into crystals. The return is made on the hillside above the valley with moorland views.

START: From the car park entrance turn left down the rough track signposted 'Falling Foss'. Cross the bridge and turn right along the path signposted 'Coast to Coast Walk'. This walk is 190 miles long and connects St Bees in Cumbria and Robin Hood's Bay. Cross the footbridge and pass Midge Hall, it was originally the old Keeper's Cottage. Falling Foss is on the left and visible through the trees.

The path climbs above the stream along a route marked with red posts. Follow the path towards Littlebeck to reach the Hermitage. This large boulder has been carved out to form a shelter, on the top of the rock are two carved stone seats. It was created by a stone mason called Jeffrey. The path descends some steps and continues through the wood passing a place where alum was quarried in the 18th and 19th centuries. You can see the friable alum shale lying around the site.

The path continues above the stream and leads to a kissing gate into the hamlet of Littlebeck. This quiet hamlet of scattered houses is shunned by many motorists because of the steep hills in and out of the valley. Turn right up the road. Just beyond the village hall turn right up the 1 in 4 hill. After half a mile, near the top of the hill, turn right along a track which passes above Thorn Hill Farm, then continue over the moor to reach a road. Turn right down the road into the wood turning left into Falling Foss car park.

Mallyan Spout

Parking: The large car park in Goathland (NZ 833013).
By Train: This walk can be reached by the North York Moors
Railway from Pickering or Grosmont. Walk up the road into
Goathland and the start of the walk is from the car park on
your right.

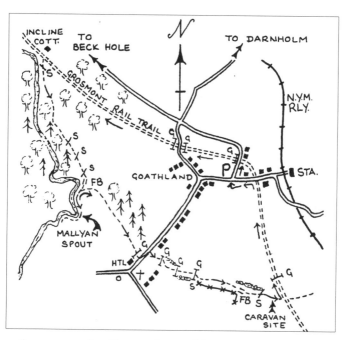

The scattered village of Goathland is picturesquely set between two streams surrounded by open moorlands. The village and its railway has been used in a number of film and TV series most notably in the Heartbeat series.

The village was served by one of the earliest and most fascinating railways in England. When the railway line was built in 1836, to a scheme devised by George Stephenson, the carriages were to be hauled by horses. On the downhill sections the horses were placed in a carriage at the back! One section of the line was too steep for horses and carriages were hauled up the slope while a tank filled with water was lowered as a counterbalance. It was 11 years later that the line was mechanised and twenty nine years after its opening that the incline was by-passed by the present deviation line to Grosmont.

This walk begins by descending this fascinating railway incline. It continues along the wooded valley formed by West Beck to reach Mallyan Spout. This is the highest of nine waterfalls which can be found around Goathland. A path then climbs up to Goathland church. The return to the car park is made along another section of the 1836 horse drawn railway line.

START: From the car park entrance turn left for 50 yards, then turn left again through a gate signposted Grosmont Rail Trail. The full four mile rail trail goes through to Grosmont where a return can be made by the railway. Our walk leaves the trail at the foot of the incline. Follow a track which passes through a gate and descends to a road. Cross straight over and continue descending the old incline until you reach Incline Cottage.

Leave the Rail Trail and turn left through a gate opposite the cottage. Follow the path over the field with West Beck on your right. The path climbs a hillside then follows the edge of the field keeping the river on your right. Three stiles and a footbridge lead down into deciduous woodland. After crossing a boardwalk a signpost indicates the way you return to Goathland but continue beside the river, crossing over boulders, to reach Mallyan Spout waterfall. It is better after rain as the small stream drops 76 feet into West Beck.

Return to the signpost you passed earlier and fork right climbing into the village by the side of the Mallyan Spout Hotel. Pass through a kissing gate. Goathland church is on your right. Bear left around the bus shelter then carry straight on over the road to a public footpath sign. Continue and pass through a metal gate and the track continues with a hedge on your left. Pass through another metal gate and the hedge continues on your right. This leads to a gate and stile, continue with a wire fence on your right. After 300 yards turn right over a stone slab foot-bridge continue with a hedge on your left to a stile which leads into a caravan site. Turn right to the caravan site entrance and turn left along the tree lined track into Goathland. This was the route of the Whitby to Pickering railway track between 1836 and 1865. When you reach the road turn left along the flagged path and turn right at the road junction back to the car park.

PICKERING AND THE MOORS

Walk 21   4 miles

Levisham Moor and
Skelton Tower

Parking: Street parking in Levisham (SE 833905).
By Train: This walk can be reached by the North York Moors
Railway from Pickering or Grosmont. From Levisham Station
walk up the road towards Levisham at the sharp bend turn left
onto the moor and begin at paragraph 3 after **START.**

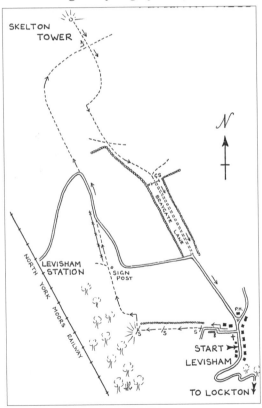

This moorland walk incorporates two fine viewpoints. Shortly after leaving Levisham the path leads over fields to a magnificent 'surprise view' into wooded Newtondale. Nestling in the bottom is Levisham Station on the North York Moors Railway which operates from Pickering to Grosmont. It has been used on a number of occasions as a location for films and television. As the path skirts the hillside you may see a steam engine hauling its carriages through the valley.

The second viewpoint is at ruined Skelton Tower. The tower was built by the Rev. Robert Skelton who was curate of Levisham from 1814-19. He built the two storey castellated stone building as a hunting lodge. Although sadly in ruins, work has been undertaken to stop any further deterioration. From the tower there is a magnificent view into Newtondale, some 150 feet below the North York Moors Railway threads its way along the steep sided valley bottom.

Levisham is an interesting village. The road runs through the centre of the village with houses standing back at either side beyond a wide green and at its head is the Horseshoe Inn. It is remote being reached from Lockton and the main Pickering-Whitby road by negotiating a very steep sided but very picturesque ravine. The road westwards beyond Levisham Station is a Forestry Commission toll road with a rough unmade surface which connects into the normal road system near Stape, north of Newton-on-Rawcliffe.

START: Walk up the village towards the Horseshoe Inn and turn left after the church along the tarmac road. Follow the road that swings to the right, then left passing a fine example of dry stone walling on your left. When the road turns sharp left carry straight on over a stile indicated by a public footpath sign. Continue over the field with a stone wall on your right. After crossing two fields you reach a stile. At this point a magnificent view opens out of Newtondale and Cropton Forest.

Follow the track to the right that skirts the hillside providing a view down to Levisham Station on the North York Moors Railway. The track descends a little but continues along the hillside eventually reaching a signpost. Continue straight ahead along a track to the 'Moor'. Keep the fence on your left and eventually you join the road which descends from Levisham village to the railway station. Continue down the unfenced moorland road.

At the long sweeping bend carry straight on along a track onto Levisham Moor, marked by a public footpath sign. (If you approach from Levisham Station turn left). Follow the track over the moor and the ruins of Skelton Tower come into view. Three-quarter of a mile from the road turn left along the path which leads to Skelton Tower. In front of the ruined building is a breathtaking view down into steep sided Newtondale.

Return along the same path but cross straight over the track you walked out on. In front of you on the hillside you should be able to see a track climbing the hillside. Your path leads over the moor and up this track. At the top bear left on the track to a wall corner, then continue with the wall on your right to a gate. Cross over a stone stile and walk down Braygate Lane. When the lane joins the road continue straight ahead into Levisham.

Walk 22

Spectacular Newtondale

Parking: Saltergate Brow car park (SE 852938) on the A 169 Pickering to Whitby road.
By Train: Begin the walk at paragraph 4 after Start. Use Newtondale Halt on the North York Moors Railway.

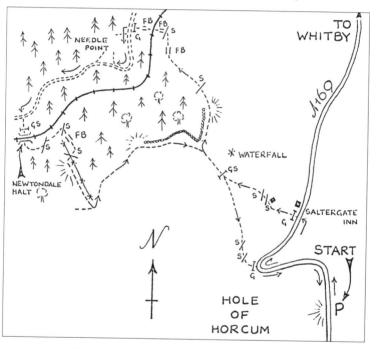

This walk passes through some spectacular scenery. After crossing Levisham Moor the descent into Newtondale is made along the side valley of Havern Beck which has a small waterfall in its upper reaches. The small stream has cut a deep valley some 200 feet below the moor top. Newtondale is a glacial overflow channel with steep wooded sides, it was cut by water escaping south after the last Ice Age. This same valley was used by George Stephenson in 1836 when he connected Whitby with Pickering by railway.

The Pickering to Whitby railway has had a fascinating history. It was originally built in 1836 to be operated with horse drawn carriages. It was taken over in 1845 by the York and North Midland Railway Company whose chairman was George Hudson, the Railway King. By 1847 the line was improved and steam engines began running. The line was closed in 1965 under the Beeching Plan but the spectacular scenery on the line brought together a dedicated band of enthusiasts to preserve the line. The trust now operates a regular service of both steam and diesel engines on the line. It is a rewarding sight to look down from the moor onto a Grosmont bound steam engine pulling its carriages up the valley.

The walk climbs steeply out of the valley from Newtondale Halt. This walk can be undertaken by taking the train from Pickering to Newtondale Halt. You pass the Hole of Horcum first and the Saltergate Inn before descending the valley of Havern Beck to return to Newtondale Halt. For all walkers there is the opportunity to extend the walk by following one of the circular waymarked trails from Newtondale Halt.

START: From the car park cross over the road to look down into the vast hollow of the Hole of Horcum. Turn right along the rim of the hollow down to the bend on Saltergate Bank. Follow the road down to the Saltergate Inn and turn left in the car park along the signposted footpath. Cross over the cattle grid, or through the gate at the side and follow the track. Pass to the left of the house and cross two stiles.

Keep the wire fence on your left until it sweeps left then continue on the track over the field to a gate and stile. As you continue on the track a ravine opens up on your right and the path sweeps right following the top edge. Looking back you can see the waterfall on Havern Beck. At a stone wall take the path to the right which descends the side of the ravine but do take care on this descent. There are spectacular views on your right.

Near the bottom of the descent cross over a stile, then continue on a path with a fence and forestry on your left and Havern

Beck on your right. Cross a footbridge and continue with the stream on your left. A stile and footbridge lead across to the North York Moors Railway line. Cross another stile and follow the track to a footbridge, then climb up the bank to a gate. Turn left on the forestry track with the conifer-clad sides of Newtondale on either side. After three-quarter of a mile you reach Newtondale Halt on your left. Turn left to the railway halt where there is a seat and local map.

From Newtondale Halt cross over a stile beside a gate and pass under the railway then turn left, there is a stream on your right and a wooden fence on your left. After 200 yards cross over a stile and continue with the fence on your right. Eventually turn right over a stile and a footbridge over Pickering Beck then continue straight ahead climbing under the trees with a fence on your right. A series of steps lead up to a seat with an excellent view along the valley. As you continue climbing you pass the sheer rock wall of Yew Tree Scar on your left and eventually arrive on the moor top.

Turn left and follow the top of the crags but don't let children stray too close to the edge along here. There are excellent views both into Newtondale and over the moors. The 'pyramid' at RAF Fylingdales can be seen on the skyline. As you approach a fence follow the track to the right heading towards the Saltergate Inn. On the left you have excellent views of the railway line threading its way through the valley below. Follow the boundary wall around until you rejoin the track you walked earlier above Havern Beck and turn right.

You can return by the route passed the Saltergate Inn, turning right up the road to the car park or as an alternative you can take the track over the moor which climbs to the bend on Saltergate Bank. The path beside the boundary fence is clearly visible from the moor. It crosses two stiles then turns left through a gate to reach the bend on Saltergate Bank. Retrace your steps above the Hole of Horcum to the car park.

The Bridestones

Parking: Street parking in Lockton, (SE 844899), off the A 169 Pickering to Whitby road.

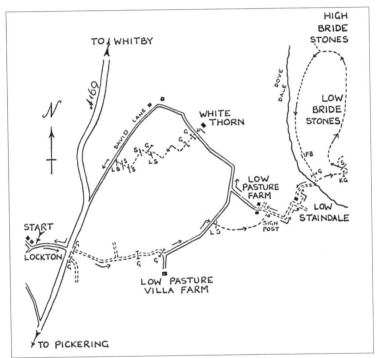

The Bridestones are rock outcrops standing on the moors above Staindale. The area is a nature reserve owned by the National Trust and managed jointly with the Yorkshire Naturalist's Trust. The main points of interest are the Low and High Bridestones, sandstone rocks which have been eroded by wind and rain into fantastic shapes. The surrounding griffs, small ravines and valleys contain many interesting plants and on the moor you may see red grouse, curlew and meadow pipit.

Although this is not the longest walk in the book it is more strenuous than other of a similar length with a number of steep climbs. The walk passes through some good deciduous woodland in an area noted for its conifer plantations and there is also a pleasant mix of moorland, rough pasture and fields. There are toilets and a picnic site near Staindale Lake before climbing up to the Bridestones.

START: From Lockton walk back along the road to the A169 and pass through the gate on the left at the opposite side of the road, signposted public footpath. There is a bench mark on the stone gate post. Walk along the stoned track with a conifer clad hillside in front of you across the valley. The track turns left and descends into mixed woodland. At the junction turn right and climb to a gate. Continue on the same track over rough pasture and at the top of the rise turn right through a gate, then walk along an access road.

After 300 yards turn right over a ladder stile and follow the path passing the farm on your left. Join a broad lane just beyond the farm and turn right. The track swings left and descends to Low Staindale. Follow the track to the right at Low Staindale then turn left passing the house on your left, then turn left and right along a broad grassy track. The track descends to a small stream which is crossed on stepping stones. At the far side of the stream note the gate on your left, this is the way you return.

Walk straight ahead with the wood on your left and pass through a kissing gate. Turn immediately left to an information board, then pass through a squeeze stile. In 15 yards fork left and follow the path which climbs through the wood. The path continues over open moor to pass the Low Bridestones. Continue along the path which bears left and descends into a small moorland gill and then climbs to the High Bridestones.

The High Bridestones are over to your right but you leave the area by turning left on a broad path. Dove Dale is on your right and the Low Bridestones are over to your left. The path descends a ridge then continues over footbridges and beside the stream to the gate you noted earlier. Fifty yards beyond the gate turn right over the stepping stones and retrace your steps passed Low

Staindale. Walk up the hill to Low Pasture Farm.

Pass between the farm buildings and at the farm entrance turn right along the road which will lead back to Lockton. Turn left opposite White Thorn through a waymarked gate and follow the waymarked route along the field edges. When you reach a gate turn left over a ladder stile, then turn right to a stile over a fence. Turn half left descending gradually down the hillside to a stile. Turn right up the field keeping the hedge on your right. Cross over a stile then a ladder stile at the end of the next field brings you into David Lane. Turn left down the lane, then left again beside the main road and finally turn right into Lockton.

Love Lane and
Little Park Wood

*Parking: The large pay and display car park near the
roundabout in Pickering (SE 799838).*

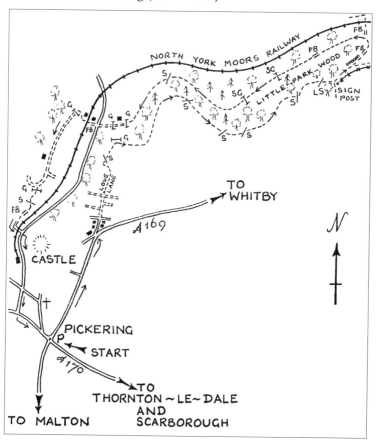

The market town of Pickering lies at the gateway to the North York Moors National Park for people travelling from the south. Among the places you can visit in the town are Pickering Castle, now in the care of English Heritage and the parish church which displays a fine set of 15th century frescoes. Other attractions include the privately run North York Moors Railway which offers steam and diesel rail services through Newtondale to Goathland and Grosmont; also of interest is the Beck Isle Museum showing everyday life of the area in the last 150 years.

The walk passes out of Pickering along Love Lane then follows the wooded valley of Pickering Beck. It descends into Little Park Wood before the return is made through the woods and along riverside paths to Newbridge. The route back to Pickering provides views of some of the rolling stock of the North York Moors Railway and also of Pickering Castle set above the town.

START: From the roundabout in Pickering walk up the Whitby road. At the top of the hill pass the road signposted to Pickering Castle on your left and take the next fork left along Love Lane, signposted as a public footpath. New houses have been built but the footpath goes straight ahead for 200 yards to reach a road. Cross straight over the road and continue on the signposted path which passes through a nursery with green-houses.

The straight broad track eventually becomes a field path. At the end of the field bear left and cross over a stile and cross the next field to a wood. Turn right in front of the gate on the path along the fieldside of the wood. There should be plenty of opportunities to see a variety of woodland birds in the deciduous trees. The path continues beside the wood crossing over a number of stiles until a ladder stile gives access into the wood.

When you reach a fence and signpost take the path to the left which descends the hillside keeping the fence on your right. Bear left when the track forks and continue downhill with a stone wall on your left. Cross a small footbridge in the bottom of the valley and continue on the path to a larger footbridge over Pickering Beck. Do not cross this bridge but turn left at the signpost. The path leads through Little Park Wood.

Cross over another small footbridge to reach a stile beside a gate. The broad path passes through a planted section of young conifers and deciduous trees to reach a stile into a field. Continue walking across the field with a wooded hillside on your left and Pickering Beck on your right.

Eventually the field narrows and you cross a stile on your left to reach the path along the bottom edge of the wooded hillside. Continue and eventually pass between some Duchy of Lancaster buildings and continue to the road. Cross over the road and take the signposted footpath on the other side. Cross over the footbridge and pass to the left of the houses. Take care when crossing the North York Moors Railway then pass the next houses on your right. At the end turn left through a gate which carries a waymarking arrow. Cross the field and continue along the bottom of the wooded hillside which is on your right.

Over to your left is rolling stock used by the North York Moors Railway. Pass a house and just beyond is a disused limekiln. The burnt lime from the kiln would have been used to sweeten the acid soils to improve the yield of the crops. Continue along the track and when it sweeps right carry straight on through a gate. Bear left across the field set in a wall beside the stream. Follow the riverside path which leads to a footbridge, continue on the other side of the river to a broad track where you turn left across the railway line to the Newbridge Road. Above you on the hillside is Pickering Castle. Turn right down the road into Pickering passing the railway station on your right and later a car park on your left. At the traffic lights turn left along Hungate back to the roundabout.

The River Derwent

Parking: The free car park in Norton, (SE 792712). From the centre of Malton take the B1248 Beverley road. Cross the river and railway crossing and immediately turn right, signposted Pocklington. Take the first turn left into St. Nicholas Street and the car park is on your left.

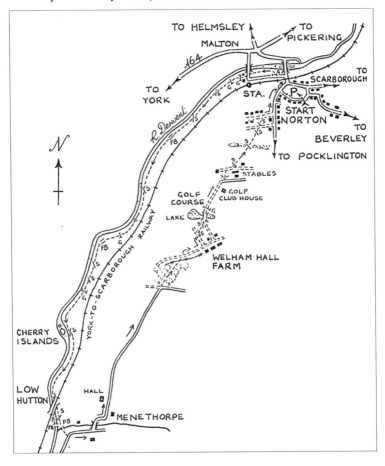

The walk follows the bank of the River Derwent from Norton to Low Hutton returning through the hamlet of Menethorpe and passes through the parkland around the former village of Welham. The return is made across a golf course, the modern equivalent of 18th century parkland.

The River Derwent has been a controversial river over the last 300 years. An Act of Parliament was obtained in 1702 to make a canal and navigable river between Scarborough Mills and the River Derwent at Hemingborough near Selby. The estimated cost was £60,000. It was 20 years later that work started, £4,000 was spent on building five locks and on removing the shallow stretches of the river which made it navigable to Malton. Lord Rockingham then sank a boat just beyond his wharf at Malton so that tolls would be paid to him as the work had been undertaken at his expense. This caused a local outcry.

It was some considerable time later that the boat was raised and the river improved to reach further wharfs in Malton. The navigable river brought goods into Malton much more cheaply due to reduced transport costs. In 1807 the Earl Fitzwilliam's candidate for one of the two Members of Parliament for the borough was defeated so he promptly raised the tolls on the river by an amount between 33% and 80%.

START: From the car park entrance turn right along St Nicholas Street. Turn right at the road junction and cross over the level crossing, then immediately turn left down Norton Road. The River Derwent is on your right. After 100 yards turn right through a gateway into a picnic site and follow the flagged path along the river bank. As you approach the bridge look for the flood markers across the river set in a brick wall. When you reach the road cross over and bear left, then turn right into the road beside the surgery which leads to a gate beside the river with a Centenary Way signpost. This is a waymarked trail between York Minster and Filey Brigg.

Continue on the track which returns to the riverside. On the opposite side of the river can be seen some of the old wharfs which are now overgrown. The walk continues alongside the river for three miles passing through a series of gates and stiles with a few sleeper footbridges over drainage ditches. Set on the ridge to the right overlooking the river are some large houses on the outskirts of Malton. To the left is the Malton-York railway line. There can be a rich variety of woodland birds on the bank as well as coot, moorhen and mute swans swimming on the river. As you approach Low Hutton pass Cherry Islands and then the large metal swing bridge built by the railway company comes into view.

You can cross the swing bridge (so named because it swings as you walk across it) to visit Low Hutton if you wish but our walk continues past the swing bridge, crossing a smaller footbridge to reach a road. Turn left and follow the road into the hamlet of Menethorpe. Beware of traffic even though this is a quiet back road. The road passes through the pretty hamlet turning left over Menethorpe Beck then climbing gently into the foothills of the Wolds.

Menethorpe Hall stands on the left as you walk up the road. As you climb the view opens out behind you over the rolling foothills of the Wolds and down into the Derwent Valley. When the road turns sharp right walk straight ahead through an avenue of trees, marked public footpath. The path begins to descend and crosses a wire fence. Keep to the edge of the field with a post and rail fence on your right. Turn left at the waymark arrows keeping a fence on your right. After 150 yards turn right over a stile and cross diagonally over the field to a stile which gives access to a stone bridge. The view from the bridge around Welham Park is delightful.

The broad track continues through a gate onto Norton golf course. Follow the track over the course, pass the club house, go through the car park and turn left over a stile near the entrance. The path passes between hedges, then you turn right towards Star Cottage where racehorses are trained. After 60 yards turn left over a stile before a bungalow. Bear right over the field to a stile and cross diagonally over the next field following the path. Cross two stiles either side of a track and continue on a path between gardens. When you reach a street bear right to the main road. Cross the road and turn left. Take the second turn right into St Nicholas Street and the car park is on your left.

AROUND KIRKBYMOORSIDE

Walk 26   **3 miles**

Kirkbymoorside's Castles

Parking: Kirkbymoorside car park, (SE 697861), near the roundabout on the A 170 Pickering to Helmsley road.

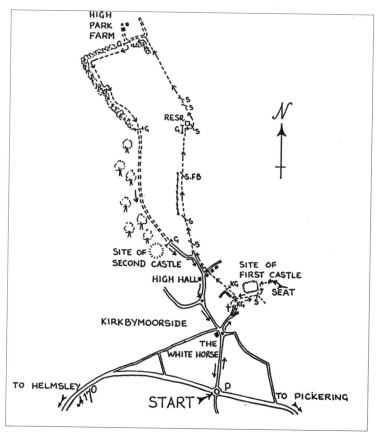

The importance of this small market town can be judged by the number of old stone waymarkers scattered over the North York Moors National Park indicating the roads to the place. In 1687 the Duke of Buckingham, who had been one of the richest men in the country, was brought to the town after falling from his horse in Tripsdale. He died in the home of the Atkinson family. It is worth while just walking around this unspoilt town and exploring its streets and houses.

Very little remains of Kirkbymoorside's two castles but it was because of its castles that it obtained a weekly market and annual fair. These were granted by the castle's owners and the place grew into a small town. The first castle to the east of the town on Vivers Hill was built in the middle of the 12th century. From the site you can look down on the town. By the late 14th century this castle had decayed. By the early 15th century the estate had passed through marriage to the Neville Family who built a new castle to the north of the town. The castle had corner towers linked by walls of which a small portion remains today.

The walk passes through the town to the medieval All Saints church that was restored in the 19th century, it was this church that gave the town its name. Paths lead to the first castle above the town, home of the de Stuteville family. A series of field paths are taken out into the countryside above the town and as you re-enter the town you pass the site of the second castle.

START: From the car park walk up the road into Kirkbymoorside. On the right you pass the unusual building with a cast iron facade inscribed "C. Carter Gas Works". At the roundabout near the White Horse Hotel fork right and walk up Church Street. Fork left passing a stone mounting block on your right. Continue for 50 yards then turn left at a sign towards the church, climb some steps to a gate into the churchyard and turn right. Keep the beech hedge on your left as you cross the churchyard and in 50 yards turn right to a kissing gate. Continue up the field to cross a stile. Turn left and follow the edge of the field round to a seat. This high ground was the site of Kirkbymoorside's first castle.

Return the way you came to the kissing gate into the churchyard and turn right keeping the churchyard wall on your left. Pass through a kissing gate and walk diagonally over the field to a gate onto a side road. Turn left for 30 yards, then turn right up Castlegate. When the road sweeps left carry straight on to two stiles. Keep the fence on your left as you leave Kirkbymoorside behind and begin walking north over the fields. After three fields you reach a reservoir, turn right for 20 yards then turn left over a stile. Follow the edge of the field to cross two more stiles close together. After crossing a further two fields turn left along a broad farm track.

Bear left at High Park Farm through a white metal gate and continue with the hedge and fence on your right. At the end of the field turn left keeping the hedge and golf course on your right. Pass through a gate and continue straight ahead on the track along the top edge of the wooded valley. As you approach the outskirts of Kirkbymoorside you reach the site of the town's second castle. Pass through the gateway and between the new houses built on the site of the castle. Follow the road to the right and descend. Fork right and pass High Hall set back from the road on your right. At the mini roundabout fork left into the town centre and continue straight ahead back down to the car park.

Sinnington Circuit

Parking: *Street parking in Sinnington off the A 170 Pickering to Helmsley road (SE 743857).*

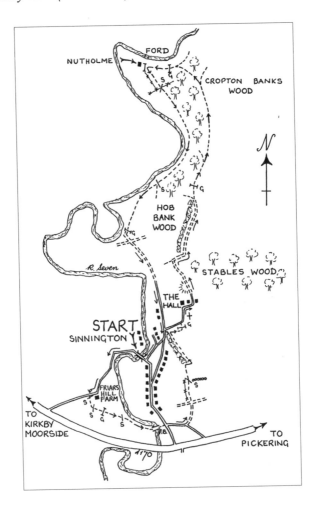

The village of Sinnington lies to the north of the Kirkbymoorside to Pickering road. Many of the stone houses stand around the spacious green with a tiny stone bridge which was once used to cross the mill stream. The small village church dates back to Saxon times but was restored in 1904. There are several ancient stones built into the walls which have served other purposes, for example there is part of a Saxon cross showing the crucifixion and another piece of a cross showing knotwork.

Close to the church the walk passes the oldest medieval building still standing in the area, apart from castles and churches. In the 12th century it was the Great Hall of the Barons de Clere who came from Rouen in France. On the eastern side of the hall there is a 12th century window; the other windows date from the 15th century.

The walk passes through Cropton Bank Wood which provides a good opportunity to see birds and grey squirrels, probably the best time being in the morning. It is worth keeping your eye open for nuthatch, treecreeper and chiffchaffs as well as the more usual woodland birds.

The walk descends to the River Seven at Nutholme. The present building carries a date of 1818 but an earlier house was the birthplace of William Scoresby on May 3rd 1760. Eventually he became the most successful whaling captain of his time sailing out of Whitby. In those days whale oil was the main source of lighting in homes and whale bones had many uses from corsets to bed bases. Probably he would remember the boyhood summers he had spent around the Seven Valley and Sinnington. For years he never saw the English summer because that was when the long voyages to the Arctic took place, returning home for the winter months.

START: From the road bridge in the centre of the village, facing upstream, turn left away from the village green. There is a footpath beside the road and the river is on your left. Pass Friars Hill Farm and turn left at the public footpath sign, cross the edge of the field keeping the farm buildings on your left. A long stile in the corner of the field crosses a gutter. Pass through a metal gate and cross diagonally across the field to a stile. Follow the path beside this pleasant section to a footbridge where you cross the river.

Walk along the side road opposite the bridge and after 100 yards turn left along a broad stoned track. Cross over a farm track and continue along the side of the field with a wire fence on your left. Cross a stile set in a stone wall and a small stone flag bridge and continue to the end of the field. Turn right for fifty yards then turn left and follow the edge of the next field to a gate at the top near the church. On reaching the road turn right, then left at the church. In front of you is the medieval, stone built Great Hall set among the farm buildings. Turn right in front of the hall and follow the concrete road around to the left, then continue straight ahead along the broad track.

As you climb past the edge of Stables Wood look back to the left into the village of Sinnington. From this point there is an extensive view over the surrounding countryside. At the end of the next field follow the indicated bridleway to the right, then turn left at the next sign on a path beside a hedge and fence. After 150 yards turn right onto a path that leads to a gate into a wood. Continue along the path on the top edge of the woodland for one mile, then take the broad track which forks left and descends through mixed woodland.

Pass through a gate into a field and continue towards the cottage of Nutholme. Turn right just before the next gate, along the wire fence, keeping it on your right. The path returns back through the woodland with the river on your right. At the end of the wood cross a stile into a field and fork right towards the river. When the river swings right continue ahead to the gate which leads to a broad track. The track climbs, crosses over another track and continues back into Sinnington where you cross over the green back to the bridge over the River Seven.

Walk 28

5.5 miles

The Woods of Kirkdale

Parking: There are wide verges in Hold Caldron Lane (SE 668859). Drive west from Kirkbymoorside on the A170 for 1.5 miles. Turn right at the signpost to Kirkdale, turn left at the T junction then take the first turn right, signposted Skiplam only. Hold Caldron Lane is the first turning right after Lund Court Farm.

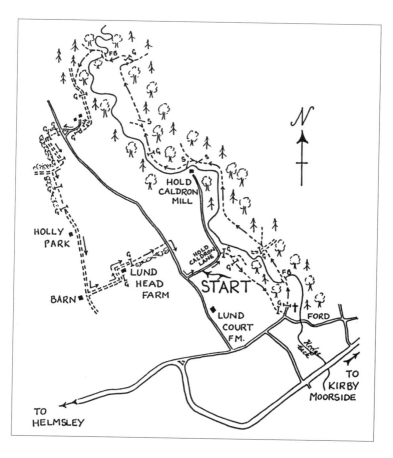

This route offers a fine woodland walk through the quiet valley of Kirkdale. The valley bottom has a series of grass fields fringed by deciduous trees while the loftier valley sides are covered by conifers. The walk passes three interesting buildings in this rural area. The first is Kirkdale Minster which dates back to Saxon times. It stands alone in this quiet peaceful valley but served a number of nearby villages and hamlets, they were Nawton, Welburn, Skiplam, Wombleton, North Holme, Muscoates and Bransdale West-side. Above the south doorway is a Saxon sundial recording the church's rebuilding by Orm in the time of Edward the Confessor 1042 -1066. A church will have stood on this site for over 1,000 years. The remoteness of the churchyard led to illicit burials of Roman Catholics in 1611.

The second building of interest on the walk is Hold Caldron Mill. The watermill was powered by Hodge Beck and was where the inhabitants of Fadmoor had their corn ground. The 1734 datestone on the building may be from an earlier mill that was incorporated into this newer building. William Baldwin was the miller in 1840. After climbing out of the valley the walk passes Skiplam Grange. It became a grange of Rievaulx Abbey in the middle of the 12th century and the last abbot of Rievaulx used to come here each summer to hunt, a right given to the grange by Henry III.

START: Walk down Hold Caldron Lane and when the road begins to descend turn right through a gate signposted public bridleway. To the left is an excellent view into Kirkdale where you will be walking later. Follow the path along the valley top, after 100 yards fork right to a gate and continue along the edge of the field with the wood on your left. After 700 yards turn left through a white gate and descend to a road junction. Turn left down the road to Kirkdale Minster standing beside Hodge Beck in its remote setting.

After visiting the church continue passing through a hunting gate and into a field. Keep the fence and wood on your left. Cross a small bridge over the river and follow the track over the field and into a wood with the stream below on your left. At the junction of tracks go straight ahead into the trees and in 15 yards fork left under beech trees. At the end of the field the path becomes a broad track which continues to Hold Caldron Mill. As you approach the mill cross a stile and pass the mill on your left.

After 70 yards fork left and cross a stile beside a gate. Follow the track over the field eventually skirting the edge of a wood on your right to reach a gate. Continue along the track and after quarter of a mile fork right over a stile opposite a belt of hawthorn trees and continue through the wood. After 600 yards turn back left through a gate marked with a sign of a man with a rucksack. This indicates the route of the Teesside Hospice Coast to Coast Walk which was created in 1991. The 154 mile walk connects Silverdale on Morecambe Bay with the South Bay at Scarborough.

Keep the old hedge on your right as you approach the river then continue to a footbridge. At the other side of Hodge Beck bear left and follow the track up the hillside. At the top of the first climb fork left and in 200 yards you join a forestry road. Continue climbing and the track eventually leads to Skiplam Grange. As you approach the farm bear left across a field to a gate into an access road. Turn left then fork right to the road.

Pass through the gate opposite and cross the field keeping the hedge on your left, pass through a gate and turn left along Guncroft Lane. Pass through a gate at the end of the lane and turn right. At the end of the field turn left and follow the hedge on your right down to Holly Park Farm. Continue down the tarmac road and turn left opposite a barn along the access road to Lund Head Farm. At the farm the access lane turns left, then right around the buildings and continues over the fields to a road. Turn right and Hold Caldron Lane is the first turning left.

Gallows Hill and Spaunton

Parking: Street parking in Lastingham (SE 728904).

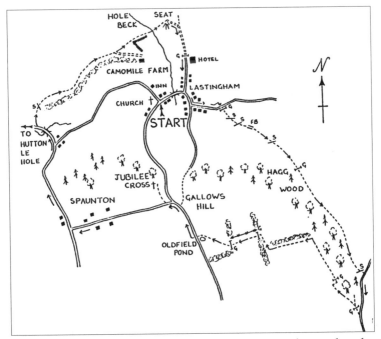

The picturesque village of Lastingham nestles under the wooded edge of the Tabular Hills with the moors climbing away to the north. The interesting church retains its 900 year old crypt which can be entered from the church by a stairway. St Cedd built a monastery here in 654 at the request of King Ethelwald. It was destroyed in the 9th century by raiding Danes but rebuilt by Benedictine monks in 1078. Gallows Hill stands to the south of Lastingham. The gallows for the Manor of Spaunton were set beneath the scarp and all gallows were usually placed beside a road to act as a warning to other wrongdoers.

The walk passes through the village of Spaunton which has declined in importance since medieval times. Then the Manor of Spaunton covered the area between the River Dove in Farndale and the River Seven which flows through Rosedale. The Manor Farm in Spaunton stands on the site of the 13th century buildings, with a Stone Age settlement below that. The Manor Court continues to function to this day. Woodman Cottage in the village is a cruck house with three bays it carries a date of 1695 but this may indicate a date when it was modernised!

START: From the road junction near the church walk along the road to Cropton. As you cross the bridge you pass St Cedd's Well on your left. Turn right, then left along the road and on the outskirts of the village pass through a gate straight in front, signposted 'public footpath'. Follow the line of trees on your right to a stile. Keep to the edge of the field to reach another stile and continue over a footbridge. Bear left along the path to another stile and continue over the field. Pass through a gate and follow the edge of the field keeping Hagg Wood on your right. At the end of the field cross over a stile beside a gate and turn right up the road. Beware of traffic.

Near the end of the wood turn right on a signposted footpath through a gate that leads into the wood. Take the track on your left which skirts the wood's edge eventually descending to turn left through a gate. Continue along the top edge of the woodland until you reach a waymarked path to the left. Cross the field keeping the hedge on your right. Turn right at the end of the field, then turn left through a gateway. Keep the fence on your right to reach a gate then bear right diagonally over the field passing Oldfield Pond to reach the road. Turn right to the road junction.

If you want a short walk take the first turn right at the junction. The path descends into Lastingham. This was the old road and Gallows Hill is on your right. When you enter Lastingham join the road through the village and turn left back to the church.

The longer walk bears left at the junction and in ten yards turn right alongside the hedge to Jubilee Cross. Here there is an excellent view with Lastingham village below and the moors stretch away beyond the village. The stone cross was erected in the 19th century to celebrate Queen Victoria's Jubilee. Retrace your steps to the road and turn right to pass through the village of Spaunton. At the end of the village turn right down the road to the junction set on unfenced roads.

Bear left along the road and cross over the bridge, after fifty yards turn right at a public footpath sign. Cross over a stile and follow the track to the right on the moorland side of the fields. When the field edge leads to Camomile Farm bear left to a field corner and continue. The path descends steeply to Hole Beck. Cross the stream on stepping stones and climb to a seat which offers an excellent view to the west. Continue bearing right to a gate. A back road then descends into Lastingham. Turn right at the road junction back over the bridge to your starting point.

ROSEDALE AND FARNDALE

Walk 30 2.5 miles

The Hidden Dale

Parking: Rosedale Abbey car park below the Milburn Arms
Hotel (SE 724959).

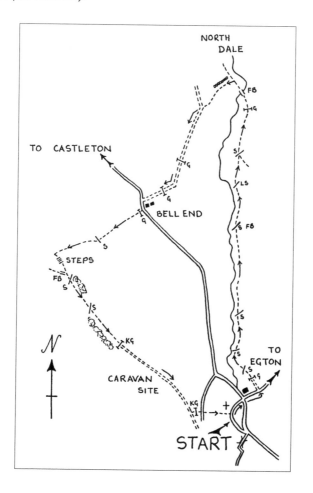

Rosedale boomed in the middle of the 19th century when iron was discovered in a number of places in the valley. Apart from the three iron mines there were calcining kilns for burning off waste material and a railway with two spurs to the mines. Tucked away off the valley of Rosedale is Northdale formed by Northdale Beck. No roads pass up the valley and many visitors are unaware that this peaceful dale exists.

START: From the green in the centre of the village walk up the road to Egton passing the entrance to the Milburn Arms Hotel. After 100 yards turn left at the public footpath sign. Cross the car park, pass through a gate and cross over the sports field. In front of you is the tree topped knoll of Hill Plantation. Cross over the stile beside the gate and continue ahead up Northdale. A series of stiles lead up the valley with Northdale Beck on your left. After three-quarter of a mile the path crosses Northdale Beck at a stone footbridge in a small wood.

At a signpost 10 yards beyond the footbridge turn left uphill with a stone wall on your right. The path continues to rise bearing left between wire fences to reach a farm road near a pond. Turn left along the farm road passing through a gate to reach the Rosedale Abbey to Castleton road. At Bell End turn left for 50 yards, then turn right at the bend through a metal gate. A public footpath sign indicates the path which gradually descends with the hedge and wall on your left to a stile.

The path continues with a fence on your left and a stream below on your right. Eventually the path descends a few steps to the left and continues down to the River Seven near a footbridge. Don't cross the footbridge but continue straight ahead to a stile and a path which climbs across a field, firstly with a hedge on your left and later on your right. Continue into a caravan site. Just beyond the kissing gate is Waterhouse Well, a stone covered water supply. Continue on the stoned road through the caravan site until you pass a children's playground, then turn left to a kissing gate that leads into Rosedale Abbey. Cross over the road and take a path past the few remains of Rosedale's Abbey on your left. Pass through two gates in front of the church and walk back into the centre of Rosedale Abbey.

Walk 31

3.5 miles

Hollins Mine

Parking: Rosedale Abbey car park. below the Milburn Arms Hotel (SE 724959).

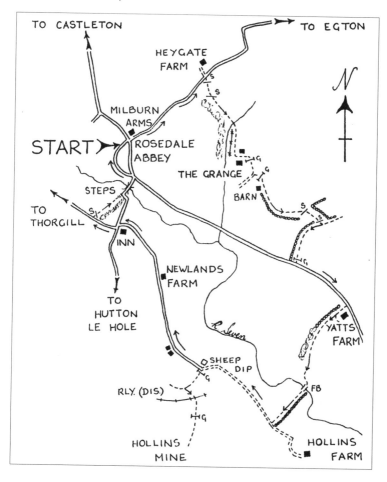

This walk passes through some interesting countryside with excellent views for most of the route. You visit Hollins Mine which was the first of three iron mines to open in the valley in 1856. The first ore was taken out on wagons but due to the poor state of the roads it was decided to build a railway. It crossed the moors from the north and reached Rosedale Abbey high on the skyline. From 1861 the ore was taken up the hillside by a rope hauled tramway and then transported over the moors to reach the foundries in Durham.

A steam boiler hauled the wagons up the incline and the local landowner required a 50ft chimney so that the smoke would not disturb his grouse. This was the famous Rosedale Chimney which was a landmark for miles around before it was demolished in 1972. The walk crosses the bottom of Rosedale Chimney Bank near the White Horse Farm Hotel. This was one of the steepest road hills in Britain at 1 in 3. In the 1920s it was used for both motor cycle and car hill climbs with only the best machines and drivers reaching the top. The steepest gradient then was 1 in 2.5

START: From the crossroads near the green in the centre of the village walk up the road to Egton, passing the entrance to the Milburn Arms Hotel. Beware of traffic as you continue up the road for 700 yards. Turn right opposite the entrance to Heygate Farm on a signposted footpath which crosses a ladder stile over a stone wall. There is an excellent view of central Rosedale at this point. Across the valley you can see the steep Rosedale Chimney Bank climbing the hillside.

Continue straight ahead down the field to a stile. Cross the next field with the hedge on your right, pass over a culverted stream at a bridge and turn right at the wire fence to the farm. Turn left, then right through a gate following the road between the farm buildings. At the end of the buildings, when the road turns right, fork left past a pond to a metal gate. Turn right passing a barn on your right and continue keeping the stone wall on your right. In the third field turn right over a ladder stile and turn left to a field corner stile with a signpost. At this point you can look across the dale to Hollins Mine and the site of the tramway, it climbs the hillside to the start of the railway which was set on the moor top where the buildings remain.

Turn right at the signpost and keep the stone wall on your right as you descend to a gate onto the road. Turn left along the road to Yatts Farm, then turn right on the signposted bridleway in front of the buildings. Fork right away from the farm buildings, keeping the wall on your right. Continue, eventually descending to a footbridge over the River Seven. Keep the broken down wall on your left as you climb to a stile with the quarry of Hollins Mine above to your right.

Turn right along the broad track and enjoy the splendid views back across the dale. Cross a cattle grid and continue along the track. Turn left through a gate opposite the sheep dip which is set within a walled enclosure. Follow the distinct track winding up the hillside and turn left at the fork to a gate. Beyond the gate you cross the bed of the tramway which was used to haul the iron ore to the railway on the moor top. Continue on the track opposite into the vast quarry of Hollins Mine.

Return back down the hillside to the broad track by the sheep dip and turn left. Eventually pass through the car park of the White Horse Farm Hotel to reach the road near the foot of Rosedale Chimney Bank. Take the road opposite signposted to Thorgill. After 150 yards turn right over a stile opposite Red House golf course on the signposted footpath. Descend, keeping the hedge on your right to a set of steps beside a house, these lead to the road. Continue over the bridge to the road junction. Turn left along the road into the village centre.

Rudland Rigg and
a Corpse Road

Parking: Low Mill car park, Farndale, (SE 672952). When the daffodils are in season an extra field is open for a small charge. At this time a one way system operates in the dale.

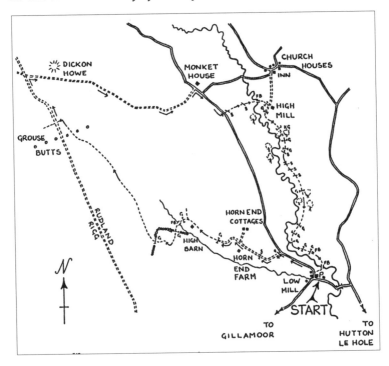

This walk passes through the remote side valley of West Gill, off Farndale. The climb onto the heather clad moors reveals excellent views. The hillside was mined in the 19th century for hard jet to supply the jet jewellery manufacturers in

Whitby. The jet was usually found along a line about 900 feet above sea level but all that remains of the industry today is a few shale heaps. Along the ridge top is the ancient road called Rudland Rigg. It was used by travellers passing between Kirkbymoorside and Stokesley and may have been in use for over 2,000 years.

The descent back into Farndale is down Monket Bank with excellent views. The route westward in Bransdale was used as a corpse road. Anyone dying in Upper Farndale was transported over the ridge to Cockayne Church in Bransdale which obtained burial rights in 1665. The route returns to Low Mill along the famous wild daffodil route beside the River Dove, the sight attracts visits from all over Britain.

START: From the car park turn right along the road up the dale for 400 yards. Beware of the traffic as the road is narrow. Turn left over a cattle grid at a sign indicating the bridleway to Rudland Rigg. Walk up the farm access road, you can see the remains of an old paved footpath in places. In front there is a good view of Horn Ridge and Horn End Crag which separate West Gill from Farndale. Cross over a cattle grid at Horn End Farm and carry straight ahead when the track bends right to Horn End Cottages. The grassy track bends right, then left, then right again to a gate. Continue along the edge of the fields, eventually keeping High Barn on your left.

Fifty yards beyond High Barn bear left at two gateposts, where a bridleway sign indicates the route. Continue with the wall on your right to a gate. Cross the footbridge over West Gill Beck and a stile leads into a field. Climb the slope to a gateway in the wall on your left. Follow the sunken track up the hillside which bears left, then swings right to a gateway. There are excellent views back into Farndale and into this side valley of West Gill.

Continue along the gently rising path which climbs the hillside to the Rudland Rigg Road on the moor top. Bracken can be a nuisance in summer but the superb views compensate. As you climb you pass through the area where the jet was mined. As you pass a line of grouse butts you can start looking left for the broad moorland track that has never been surfaced. When you reach the road bear right. The track you have just taken was used as a short cut for waggoners wanting to be into the southern part of Farndale until a landslip swept away part of the route.

Continue along Rudland Rigg for half a mile and turn right at a crossroads of tracks. Follow the broad track over the moor passing Dicken Howe on your left. This was the track used by traffic passing between Farndale and Bransdale including coffins carrying the dead for burial in Cockayne churchyard. Eventually the track begins to fall away more steeply and an excellent view opens out into Upper Farndale. This area was the part of the dale that the water authorities wanted to flood and turn into a reservoir for Hull.

The broad track descends steeply into Farndale joining a tarmac road at Monket House. Turn right passing straight over a road junction and after 150 yards turn left over a stile signposted 'Public footpath to Churchhouses'. Descend along the edge of the field crossing another stile to reach a footbridge over the River Dove. At the far side turn right over the field to a gate. Turn right along the track and pass between the buildings of High Mill.

Continue through the gate and cross the field to two stone posts. Follow the distinct path down the dale with the River Dove on your right. This is part of the famous daffodil walk between Churchhouses and Low Mill. which now forms part of the Farndale Nature Reserve. After a mile you reach a footbridge where you turn right along a path that leads to the road where you turn left back into the car park.

Lowna and the River Dove

Parking: Lowna car park (SE 685910). From Hutton le Hole take the road north to Castleton. Take the first turn left to Gillamoor. After a mile cross a bridge and in 200 yards turn right into a small car park.

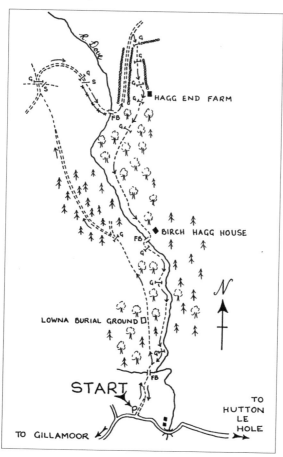

The mill in the small hamlet of Lowna was used for fulling in the 17th and 18th centuries, it stands just upstream of the road bridge. Fulling mills pounded the new woollen cloth to remove grease and force the wool strands into a stronger cloth. Later the mill became a tannery. Copious supplies of water were required for tanning hide. This was run off from the river and diverted along water channels to various steeping pits inside the mill, here the hides were steeped in solutions of various strengths of water and tree bark. When the tanning was completed the hides were dried in sheds with louvered doors to allow a movement of air; these can still be seen.

The walk passes the Society of Friends burial ground at Lowna. A ford at Lowna is associated with the death of Sarkless Kitty. The girl may have committed suicide over a love affair and local people began seeing her ghost — sarkless, naked without a petticoat at the ford. Because she may have committed suicide she couldn't be buried in the churchyard but her body disappeared. It is now believed that a local couple who had lost a daughter of about the same age buried Sarkless Kitty's body with their daughter in Lowna burial ground.

START: From the end of the car park follow the track that eventually descends to a footbridge. Follow the track to the right, then fork left along the path signposted 'Low Mill via Park Farm'. After 200 yards you pass the dry stone wall enclosure around Lowna Burial Ground on your left. Continue along the hollow way with a wall on your right to a gate which leads to a broad track, this climbs gently through the forestry.

When you leave the wood continue ahead on the track until you reach a farm road. There are some pleasant views to the right as you cross over the moor. At the farm road turn right over the moor to a stile beside a gate. The right of way should go straight down the hillside but it has been planted with young trees. The easiest way is to follow the broad track which passes through the gate, it takes an easier gradient down the hill then turns back right to another stile beside a gate.

Follow the wire fence on your right and eventually it swings left and descends to a footbridge over the River Dove. Bear left up a track between stone walls. When you reach the stream turn back right through a gateway in a stone wall. Cross the field to a gate, then keep the wall on your left to pass below Hagg End Farm. The farm carries a carved stone with DJ 1897. This may commemorate Queen Victoria's Diamond Jubilee in 1897. The track continues along the edge of the field to a gate. Cross the next field to a gate that leads to a delightful woodland path.

The path leads down towards the river and passes in front of Birch Hagg House. Turn right over the footbridge and left through a gate. The riverside path you now follow has one of the finest displays of wild daffodils when they are in bloom. Keep the riverside on your left until you swing right to the footbridge you crossed near the start. Turn left over the bridge and climb back to the car park.

AROUND HELMSLEY

Walk 34   4.25 miles

Nunnington Hall and Caukleys Lane

Parking: Street parking in Nunnington (SE 668794). Take the Thirsk road out of Helmsley. After a mile turn left on the B1257 Malton Road, after 3 miles turn left to Nunnington.

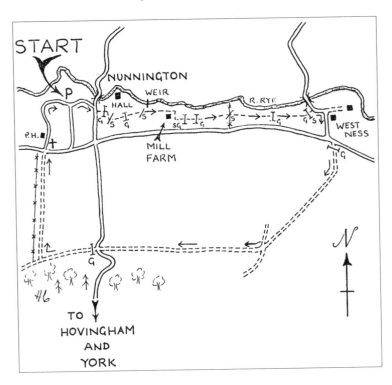

According to local legend Nunnington Hall stands on the site of a nunnery suppressed at the beginning of the 13th century for immorality. The present hall dates back to the 16th century and stands in a delightful setting beside the River Rye. Inside the building there are panelled rooms, a Great Staircase, Dining Room, Oak Hall and bedrooms all interestingly furnished with paintings, furniture and other household items of the appropriate period. In the attic, which was the servants quarters is the Carlisle Collection of 22 miniature rooms each reduced to one eighth normal size. The collection took forty years to build and amass. There are also beautiful gardens patrolled by peacocks and a wooded stretch near the river. The building is run by the National Trust and is open on various days each week between Easter and October.

The walk crosses the fields beside the River Rye to reach the hamlet of West Ness. Caulkleys Lane is followed climbing to a point on Caukleys Bank above Nunnington with excellent views before you drop back into the village. Caukleys Lane provides an opportunity in summer to identify numerous wild flowers and butterflies. We found field bindweed, field scabious, weld, lady's bedstraw, knapweed, meadow cranesbill, purple vetch, birdsfoot trefoil, harebells and both scentless and pineapple mayweed.

START: From the road bridge near Nunnington Hall walk up the road signposted Hovingham and York. After 100 yards turn left at the public footpath sign. As you walk along the stoned track there are views of Nunnington Hall and grounds on your left. Pass through a gate and turn right on a grass path to a stile. Turn left beside a walled embankment and ditch; these garden features are called a haha. Continue straight across the field to a gate, then cross the next field to a stile beside the river.

At the other side of the stile is a seat overlooking a weir. This was the point where water was taken off to power Nunnington Mill. Following the line of trees over the field you can see the mill leat on your right which carried the water. In 1890 the mill was operated by Christopher Foxton who was also a corn factor. The large building was probably used for storing corn as well as milling. Walk past the mill and immediately turn right; you can see the mill wheel still in position.

Continue for 25 yards then turn left to a gate and stile. Continue ahead along the edge of the field to a gate, then cross the next field. Two thirds of the way over the field the edge of the field bears to the left but the path carries straight on to a stile. Follow the line of trees to a hunting gate, then continue along the edge of the fields with the wooded banks of the River Rye on your left.

As you approach the road bear left to a stile beside a gate. Turn right along the road passing through the hamlet of West Ness. Turn right at the junction. The broad grass verges beside the road lead up to a T junction. Turn left for 15 yards, then turn right at the public bridleway sign stating 'Caulkleys Lane'. This beautiful green lane climbs steadily upwards, offering an improving view as you approach the top. In summer the lane has a wide variety of wild flowers to identify. Eventually the lane crosses a stoned track. Continue straight ahead and rejoin the lane at the other side.

As you walk along the ridge there are extensive views southwards to Hovingham and the wooded ridges of the Howardian Hills. To the north across the valley of the River Rye are the North York Moors. When you reach the road, there are two seats on your right. Continue straight over the road where the track continues ahead. At the end of the first field on your right, turn right along a broad path with a fence on your left. The path descends to a road junction near Nunnington Church. The earliest parts of the church date back to the 12th century. Continue straight ahead passing the Royal Oak Inn (or maybe stepping inside for refreshment) and other stone cottages in the village. At the bottom of the road turn right back along the road to the bridge.

Walk 35

5.25 miles

Cow House Bank

Parking: From Helmsley take the Carlton Road which turns left
on the eastern outskirts of the town. After 3 miles park in the
car park on the left before the road descends Cow House Bank
(SE 612886).

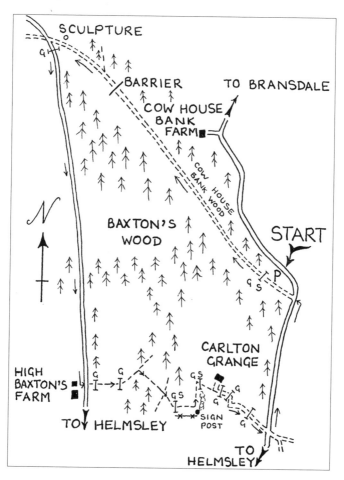

The route finding on this walk is relatively easy. From the car park there is an extensive view northwards over the small fields and rough pasture to the heather moorlands beyond. The first part of the walk is along a forestry road but the forestry is varied in size and not a regulation uniformity. At Roppa Edge you encounter a sculpture of an eight feet high irregular shaped aluminium ring. It was one of two set up on this site, the other has been vandalised. The work was commissioned in 1975 by the Yorkshire Arts Association from Austin Wright, a sculptor who lived near York. Both the modern design of the sculpture and its siting caused controversy before it was erected on this plateau edge.

There is an extensive view northwards over Helmsley Moor and Bilsdale East Moor with remote Bransdale over to the right. The viewpoint and its surrounding moorland can be a rich source of birds of prey in winter. The return is made down the quiet road to High Baxton's Farm and finally across the woods and fields on a track also used by walkers on the 154 mile Teesside Hospice Coast to Coast Walk.

START: From the car park walk over to the edge of the plateau and take in the extensive view northwards, it covers Helmsley Moor and Pockley Moor. The view to the right ends in the ridge of Birk Nab with Birk Nab Farm nestling on the hillside. Turn away from the cliff top and turn right along the broad forestry track. Pass over a stile beside the gate and continue along the broad track, which gently rises, for one and a half miles. Over to the right there are occasional views through the trees of Helmsley Moor extending to the horizon.

Eventually you pass through a barrier and continue over the moor to join a minor road near the aluminium sculpture. There is an extensive view northwards at this point. Turn left down the road which is gated at this point. On your left is Baxton's Wood and on the right is Helmsley Moor. The road continues down Baxton's Rigg for one and a half miles and for half this distance is unfenced with occasional trees to the left, the remains of a former plantation which may have been planted as a windbreak.

Turn left opposite High Baxton's Farm along the signposted

footpath. Pass through a gate and follow the broad farm track across the edge of the field, then pass through another gate into a wood. The yellow sign on the gatepost of a man carrying a rucksack indicates the path is also used by walkers on the Teesside Hospice Coast to Coast Walk.

Follow the track in the wood to the left and after 70 yards fork right down a small valley. This descends to a point where tracks cross; take the one opposite which bears right up the wooded hillside. Cross over the stile beside the gate and keep the wire fence on your right. At the end of the field, turn left at the sign-post and keep the hedge on your right until you reach a stile beside a gate. Turn right over the stile and along the path past Carlton Grange. Pass through a gate just beyond the farm, then continue through gates along the farm access road until you reach the road. Turn left up the road for three-quarter of a mile, then bear left back to the car park and picnic site.

Ash Dale and Beck Dale

Parking: Cleveland Way long stay car park, Helmsley (SE 610838). There is a two hour limit on cars parked in the Market Place.

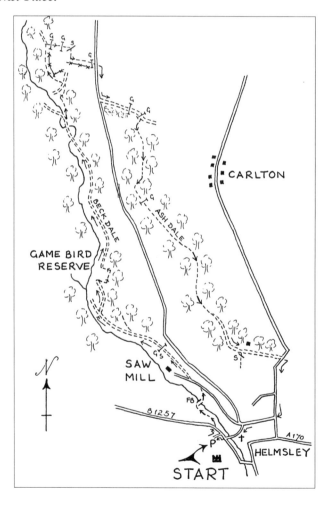

The small market town of Helmsley lies under the southern edge of the North York Moors. There is a spacious Market Place and over to the west stands Helmsley Castle. The castle was made uninhabitable after a Civil War siege but parts of the keep and buildings remain along with the massive defensive mounds and ditches. It is now in the care of English Heritage and there may be special events at certain times of the year. Nearby Duncombe Park is open to the public. The house was built in 1713 for Thomas Duncombe and now contains a 30 acre garden set among 300 acres of parkland.

To the north of Helmsley lies two wooded valleys, Beck Dale and Ash Dale. The walk provides the opportunity to identify a variety of birds and wild flowers. In August there was brambles and wild strawberries to sample and the flowers included eyebright, weld, harebells, lords and ladies with their orange berries, meadow cranesbill, the ubiquitous rosebay willow herb, self heal and herb robert to name just a few.

After 2.5 miles of walking up Beck Dale you climb out of the valley and cross over the fields to descend into Ash Dale for the return to the outskirts of Helmsley. The route over the fields is also used by walkers on the Teesside Hospice Coast to Coast walk. Three other long distance walks meet in Helmsley. The Cleveland Way long distance footpath begins in the Market Place. The Cleveland Way Missing Link returns to the Market Place from the coast near Scarborough. The other walk is the Ebor Way which sets out from Helmsley on its 70 mile route to Ilkley in the Yorkshire Dales.

START: From the car park walk down the Cleveland Way approach road and turn left beside the main road. Continue on the footpath until the road sweeps left and begins to climb out of the town; at this point cross over the road and take the signposted footpath beside the stream. Turn right over a footbridge and continue on the path to a broad road. Bear left along the concrete road and fork to the right at the sawmill. The broad track leads to a gate with a stile on the right. Continue on the broad track along the bottom of Beck Dale with the wooded hillside gradually growing higher.

Three-quarter of a mile beyond the sawmill, the track forks, bear right. Eventually you reach a fenced off area where game birds are bred. Turn right, then left around the perimeter fence to rejoin the broad track at the far side of the reserve. The wooded heights are now closing in on you as the valley narrows. Cross a narrow stream twice and when the stone track bears left and starts to climb the hillside, carry straight on along the narrower path along the dale bottom. After crossing a short boggy section the path bears right and begins to climb up the valley side.

As you approach the top of the valley another track merges from the left. At this point you turn left on a path that passes through young trees and is parallel with fields on your right. The woodland path then winds its way beneath more mature trees and although, in summer, bracken may be a problem the path should still be visible. When you reach a large grassy track turn right to a gate and follow the edge of the field with the fence on your left. Cross two fields and at the signpost beyond the stile turn right. There are extensive views to the south. At the end of the field turn left keeping the fence on your right till you reach a minor road.

Turn right down the road. At the end of the field on your left turn left at the public footpath sign and continue keeping the hedge on your right. The broad track passes through two gates and descends into a wooded valley. In the valley bottom turn right on a path that remains in the valley, do not follow the track up the other side. The track becomes clearer as you descend Ash Dale. As the path continues beneath the wooded valley sides there is plenty of opportunity to identify a large variety of flowers.

After two miles of easy walking the track leads to a road on the outskirts of Helmsley. Turn right and you can see the keep of Helmsley Castle in front of you. Take the second turn right, just beyond the Health Centre, along Carlton Road. Follow the road when it sweeps left and pass the church on your left. At the main road turn right and left along Cleveland Way back to the car park.

Byland Abbey and Wass

Parking: From the village of Ampleforth drive west on the road to Wass. After 600 yards there are two small car parking areas to the left of the road. (SE 573786).

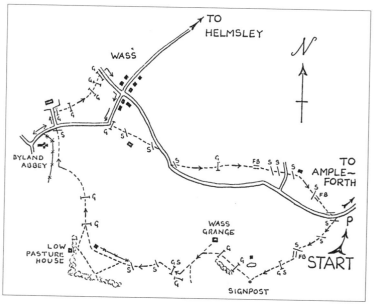

This pleasant walk passes beneath the southern edge of the Hambleton Hills and, throughout the walk, the tree clad hillsides are visible to the north. Approaching Byland Abbey the Kilburn White Horse hill carving comes into view at the same time as the abbey ruins. The walk passes through the small village of Wass which lies at the foot of the Hambleton Hills and the return is made along the edge of the hills with views to the south.

The only trouble that Byland Abbey saw before its dissolution in 1540 was in 1322. Edward II had made a raid into Scotland in retaliation for a Scottish raid into Cumbria. When the English forces retreated back to Byland Abbey they were pursued by Scottish forces. The English forces were defending the high ground towards Kilburn White Horse but the Scottish forces outflanked the English and routed them. Edward II took flight to York leaving Byland Abbey to defend itself from the raiding Scots. The building is now in the care of English Heritage and enough of the building remains to gauge its magnificence.

START: From the parking space walk down the hill in the direction of Wass. After 50 yards turn left at the public footpath sign over a stile. Walk down the field to a fence corner and continue bearing right to a stile. Continue straight ahead descending the field to a stile and footbridge. Bear right on the track over the field to a stile beside a gate. Bear left and climb up the hillside to a signpost where you bear right to a gate keeping the fence on your left. There is a pond and barn over to the right.

Continue over the next field keeping the hedge on your left. There are pleasant views on your right of the wooded slopes of the Hambleton Hills. Cross a stile beside a gate and carry straight on passing ivy covered Wass Grange over to the right. Turn left onto a track to a signpost. Continue straight ahead over the field forking right towards a gate, then turn right beside the hedge to a blue gate and cross the stile.

Continue with the hedge on your left. The Kilburn White Horse comes into view on the hillside then the ruins of Byland Abbey. After 100 yards turn left over a stile and continue walking with the hedge on your right for 50 yards. Bear left across the field at a signpost to reach a stile, then continue with the fence on your right.

The easiest way from here is to continue on the ridge to a ruined building, keeping the fence on your right. Then turn right and descend to a gate. The farmer prefers people to use this route but the right of way goes a different way. It descends the hillside to the left down to the hedge and then turns right to a field corner. It then heads towards Low Pasture Farm but turns right around the garden hedge and crosses the field to the same gate mentioned in the preferred route.

Pass through the gate and cross the field to a gateway, bear left on an indistinct path until you reach the boundary fence of the ruins of Byland Abbey which are ahead. Turn right along the boundary fence and cross the field to reach a stile onto the road. The walk continues straight ahead up the access road to Abbey House but if you wish to visit Byland Abbey and the Abbey Inn turn left to the entrance.

Retrace your steps from Byland Abbey and turn left along the access road to Abbey House. Turn right through a gate before the buildings and walk on to a gate at the end of the field. Bear left as you cross the next field to a gate in the top corner of the field. Bear left to a gate and continue walking to another gate which leads into a minor road. Turn right and walk down to the crossroads in Wass, the Wombwell Arms is set at the other side of the road. Turn right down the road through the village. It is worth examining the older stone cottages to see if there are indications of whether they were built with stone from Byland Abbey. In the 17th and 18th centuries ruined abbeys were considered a good source of building stone.

When the road turns right towards Byland Abbey turn left through the gate at the public footpath sign. After 50 yards turn left over a stile then bear right over the field. Pass to the left of an electric pole and climb to a stile onto the road near the field corner. Turn right beside the road for 200 yards then turn left over a stile at the public footpath sign. Walk along the track over the field, pass through a gate and continue over the next field to a footbridge. Continue on the path to two stiles and cross an access road. Climb to a stile at the top of the field and pass a wooden shack on your left. Keep the fence on your left to reach a stile and footbridge, pass through some scrub and gorse to a stile which leads onto a road. Turn left up the hill back to the parking space.

THE HAMBLETON HILLS

Walk 38   4.75 miles

Cold Kirby and Scawton

Parking: Street parking in Cold Kirby (SE 532845). From Helmsley take the A170 Thirsk road and turn right near the top of Sutton Bank to Cold Kirby.

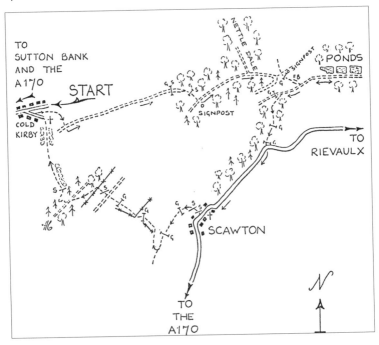

The walk starts in the small village of Cold Kirby and follows the Cleveland Way long distance footpath down into wooded Flassendale and Nettledale. A series of ponds may have mallard, moorhens or tufted duck with a chance of other wildfowl, the surrounding woods can provide a wide variety of birds including pied flycatchers, chiffchaff and nuthatch. A climb back onto the Hambleton Hills leads to Scawton. From this village you return to Cold Kirby through a wooded valley and over hill top fields with some wide reaching views.

The scattered village of Scawton stands on the plateau formed by the Hambleton Hills and surrounded by wooded valleys. The church has served the needs of the local community since the 12th century and is clean and simple in appearance. There is a piscina, a stone basin for the water which was used to wash the sacred vessels. There is also a sedilia in the chancel, a seat cut in the wall for the priest. A pillared stone carving in the chancel may have come from the nearby abbey at either Rievaulx or Byland.

In the church entrance is a reminder of a local tragedy. A bronze plaque commemorates the French crew of a Handley Page Halifax. They were killed when it crashed nearby on the 15th March 1945 returning from an operational flight. Those who died were the pilot, navigator, bomb aimer, wireless operator and gunner.

START: The village of Cold Kirby comprises a pleasant group of stone houses fronted by dry stone walls. Take the road which leads towards the church, but before you reach the church fork left at the wooden Cleveland Way sign. The path descends into a small valley. Follow the path to the right, then climb to a wooden signpost where you turn left along a stoned track. This is Low Field Lane which offers an extensive view over the countryside.

Eventually the track leads to a gate and stile. Continue down the field, keeping the hedge on your right and this leads to a path into a wooded valley. At the bottom of the path turn left along the forestry track. At the junction of tracks in Nettledale turn right. After 400 yards, when the track sweeps right, turn left and in ten yards turn right to a gate and Cleveland Way sign. Cross the footbridge and continue to the stoned track.

At this point look towards the gate on your right and note the grassy track that climbs away to its left. This is the track you will take to Scawton. First, turn left along the stone track for 500 yards if you wish to see the ponds on your left for bird life. Return and take the grassy track which climbs to the left of the gate. This distinct path climbs beneath oak trees passing through two gates to reach a road. Continue straight ahead up the road into Scawton. The church is on your left.

In the village turn right over the stile near the telephone box. Cross a second stile into a field and after twenty yards turn left to a gate. Continue walking below the farm buildings until you join a track that leads to a gate. Follow the track into a small valley where you swing sharp right, keeping the wood on your right. When the track swings left carry straight ahead through a gateway and turn left keeping the fence on your left. Pass through a gate and cross a wooden fence then continue straight ahead keeping the wire fence on your left. There are extensive views to your right.

Pass through the gate at the end of the field and continue, cross over a broad stoned access road and cross the stile opposite. Walk straight over the field to a large tree and cross the fence just behind. Turn left for 40 yards and follow the path as it bears right and begins to descend steeply into the tree covered valley. When you reach the bottom of the dale turn left for thirty yards. Turn right up the indistinct path which almost immediately bears left beneath the trees then sweeps right and follows a distinct cleared line through the wood. Climb to the top of the valley and cross the stile into a field. Continue walking ahead keeping the hedge on your right. Cross the next field to a hedged lane and continue straight ahead, passing the church on your right, into Cold Kirby.

3.25 miles

Lake Gormire and Hambleton Down

Parking: The large car park at the top of Sutton Bank on the A170 Helmsley to Thirsk road. (SE 515830).

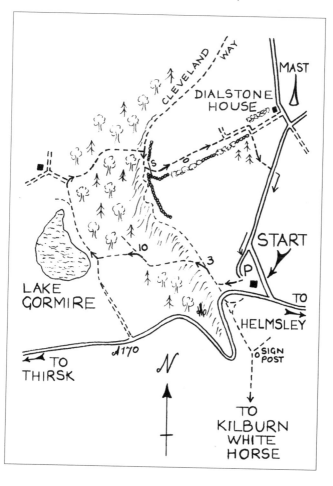

At the top of the Sutton Bank where the A 170 climbs steeply onto the Hambleton Hills there are two large car parks. Set between the car parks is the National Park Information Centre. Part of this walk coincides with the Garbutt Wood Nature Trail and you may wish to purchase a descriptive leaflet to the trail from the centre. At the top of the hill, to the south of the road there is a view indicator and a telescope. The view is extensive looking across the Vale of York to the Yorkshire Dales in the distance. Beneath you the road drops away some 500 feet into the broad valley.

The walk starts off along the Cleveland Way long distance footpath then descends steeply on the nature trail to Lake Gormire which has no feeder or exit streams. According to legend it is bottomless. The path climbs back through the crags to the Cleveland Way on the cliff top then passes over the plateau to the east which is called Hambleton Down before returning to the top of Sutton Bank.

Horses are still trained on the downs but the place reached its peak in the 18th century when it began to rival Newmarket. In 1714 Queen Anne presented a gold cup as the prize in one event. Five years later the largest field of horses ever entered for a horse race up to that time, 31 runners, competed for His Majesty's Gold Cup presented by George I. The trophy was valued at 100 guineas and was won by the Duke of Rutland's horse Bonny Black. The course eventually declined in favour of York which could offer more facilities.

START: From the car park walk over to the top of Sutton Bank and take the broad track along the cliff top on your right, signposted public footpath. Bear right at the Cleveland Way sign in twenty yards. There is a magnificent prospect showing Lake Gormire at the foot of the cliffs and the patchwork of fields extending to Thirsk and beyond. Looking back you can see Hood Hill and the crags of Roulston Scar.

After quarter of a mile fork left past number 3 post on the nature trail. The path descends towards Lake Gormire passing through the trees on the hillside. From this area a soft sandstone was quarried for donkey stones, these were sold to housewives to leave a yellow edge on there newly cleaned steps. Pass a large stone at post number 7 and at post 10 fork left on the path down to Lake Gormire. Turn right along the path on the lake shore. Fork right after 200 yards and follow the wooden catwalks along the muddy parts. At the T junction before Southwood Lodge turn right uphill. The old hollow way has been worn out by the traffic which has used it over many years.

The path climbs steeply — where it is muddy in the bottom the path has used the higher edges. Eventually you leave the wood and there is a small cliff in front of you. The path bears left along the edge of the wood and climbs the side of the cliff to join the Cleveland Way path on the top. There is a magnificent view on your left with Thirlby and Boltby beneath you.

Turn right along the Cleveland Way cliff top path for 70 yards. Near the end of the field on your left pass over a ladder stile on your left. Walk along the edge of the field with a stone wall on your right. Pass a wood and you have a choice of routes. You can continue along the lane to Dialstone Farm, this was once an inn on the Hambleton Drove road which served Scottish drovers taking their cattle south to the English markets. You can then turn right down the unfenced road over Hambleton Down to return to the car park.

The alternative route turns right at the wood and crosses Hambleton Down to the road. Here you turn right down the same road to reach the car park beside the main road.

Hawnby Hill

Parking: Take the B1257 Stokesley road from Helmsley and turn left to Hawnby. From the village follow the signs to Osmotherley. After 1.25 miles there is parking just beyond the cattle grid (SE 539917).

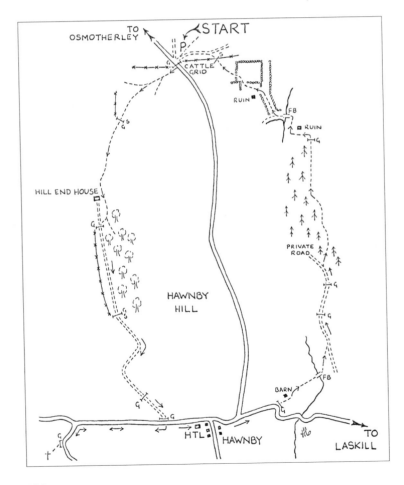

When looking northwards from the Helmsley to Sutton Bank road, or other places on the Hambleton Hills, two hills nestling side by side stand out. Rising some 500 feet from the surrounding countryside Hawnby Hill and Easterside are prominent landmarks. This walk skirts the western edge of Hawnby Hill and then descends to the small church at Hawnby which nestles in the valley beside the River Rye. After passing through Hawnby village the walk follows the western flank of Easterside to complete a circuit of Hawnby Hill.

A notice in Hawnby church states that there are no priceless treasures but there is a wealth of history. The church is old having 12th century doorways and was restored in the 14th century, possibly after being damaged by a raiding party of Scots. The church also contains a number of interesting items from more modern times. A framed newspaper cutting hangs on the wall listing 55 men of the surrounding area who had given their lives in the First World War by the 23rd October 1916. A high mortality rate for this sparsely populated area. There is a beautiful stained glass window showing a stretcher bearer carrying a casualty over the war-damaged terrain of northern France or Belgium. Another stained glass window commemorates the three sons of the rector of the church who were killed in 1917 and 1918. A third window is dedicated to 2nd Lt. Frederick William Orrey who died of his wounds near Ypres, in Belgium in 1917.

START: From the cattle grid take the signposted public bridleway which is on your right when facing towards Hawnby. Ignore the first fork on your left which is a path that is not a right of way, it heads towards the top of Hawnby Hill. Take the next fork left on the path that skirts around the edge of Hawnby Hill. On the way you pass the remains of two cairns, you can rebuild the pile of stones if you wish. You will come across these cairns all over the open moors they act as guides to the paths. Eventually the path meets a wire boundary fence and then passes over a stile beside a gate. Continue with the fence on your left and as you approach Hill End House bear left around the buildings where the broad track continues to a gate.

Walk through the edge of the wood and follow the track as it sweeps right, then left, eventually passing through a gate onto the road. Turn right down the road and fork left to the church in its delightful setting beside the River Rye. After visiting the church retrace your steps back up the road, passing the point where you joined it and continue into Hawnby village. The Hawnby Hotel is on the right.

Carry straight on at the road junction along the Osmotherley road. Then turn right on the road to Laskill. As you descend there is an excellent view of Easterside Hill. When the road sweeps right pass through a gate in front of you, then bear left passing a ruined barn. An overgrown track leads down into a field which you cross to a footbridge over Ladhill Gill. Turn left after the footbridge and continue until you merge with a stoned road. Walk along the gradually climbing access road for 300 yards, pass through two gates and fork right on an indicated footpath when you reach a private road sign.

The path climbs beneath the trees and then levels out towards the top edge of the wood. When you pass a clearing on your left you have a good view of Hawnby Hill which you have now nearly circumnavigated. Eventually a gate gives access into a field. Bear left and descend, pass a ruined building on your right and some twenty yards later turn right on an indistinct path. Keep the stream on your left to reach a footbridge. Cross over and keep straight ahead for 100 yards along an old lane then fork right up a track which may be wet. Keep to the left hand side and when you see a ruined building in the field on your left bear left, above the ruin, to two gateways set in stone walls. Cross over the rough pasture to a stile onto a rough road then turn left back to the car park.

Walk 41

Hazel Head and
Hawnby Moor

Parking: *From Helmsley take the Stokesley Road turning left to*
Hawnby. Take the Osmotherley road from Hawnby for 2.5
miles to Hazel Head car park (SE528929).

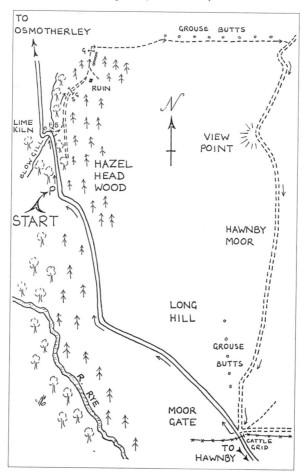

The walk visits an old lime kiln and passes through woodland before climbing onto the wide expanse of Hawnby Moor. There are excellent views throughout the walk and the best time of the year would be August and September when the heather is in bloom. The heather is a managed environment with sections of the moor being burnt off in rotation to allow young heather shoots to grow for the young grouse. Some older dense heather is retained for nesting and ground cover for the birds.

The lime kiln would have been used in the 19th century to improve the acid moors by applying alkaline lime, it would have been ploughed in to give better and more varied crops on the sweetened land. Limestone would have been brought by horse and cart from quarries on the southern edge of the North York Moors. The limestone would have been placed in the kiln separated by layers of heather or moorland coal. The kiln would be lit and the heat would then crumble the limestone to powder, this would then be raked from the bottom of the kiln. Further layers of limestone and moorland coal would have been added at the top while the kiln was burning until enough lime was produced for the farmer's needs.

START: From the car park walk along the road towards Osmotherley. The pleasant wooded section descends to a Z bend over Blow Gill. Note the signposted footpath on the right. Blow Gill merges nearby with Wheat Beck and Locker Beck to form the River Rye. Set just beyond Blow Gill is the stone built lime kiln used for preparing lime for spreading on the fields.

After looking at the lime kiln, return and cross over the footbridge over Blow Gill. Turn left and climb up the path beneath the trees until you reach a broader path. Turn left and continue climbing to reach a gate and stile. The path continues ahead passing through the wood, it then bears left passing a ruined building on your right. The path leads into a small field and then you bear left on a yellow waymarked path that leads back into the wood. Continue with a stone wall on your right until you reach a gate out of the wood onto the heather and bracken covered moors.

Walk onto the moors for about 10-15 yards then turn right on a path that leads through the heather. You climb steadily keeping the edge of the wood on your right and a line of shooting butts on your left, behind you is Black Hambleton. The 1,309 feet high hill is crossed by the ancient Hambleton Street trackway which may date back to prehistoric times. It was used regularly as a drove road for cattle in the 18th and 19th centuries being taken south from Scotland to the English markets.

The path merges in with a track beside the shooting butts and continues to join a stony track over Hawnby Moor. Turn right along the broad track. As you walk down towards Moor Gate there are excellent views especially when the heather is in bloom. To the south are the two hogsback hills of Easterside on the left and Hawnby Hill on the right. The path eventually joins the tarmac road at Moor Gate which is the start of Walk 40. Here you turn right beside the unfenced moorland road eventually descending through Hazel Head Wood back to the car park at Hazel Head.

The Osmotherley Circuit

Parking: Street parking in Osmotherley (SE 456973). The village is one mile east of the A19 Thirsk to Middlesbrough road.

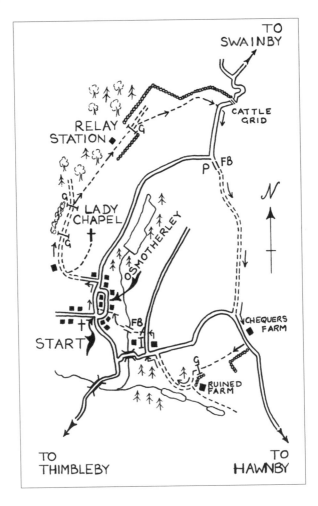

The picturesque village of Osmotherley stands on the edge of the North York Moors overlooking the Cleveland Plain and the Vale of York some 400 feet below. The heather moors stretch away to the east for some forty miles until they reach the North Sea around Robin Hood's Bay and Ravenscar. The stone houses are collected alongside the three roads into the village which meet at the market cross and barter table. The table is a slab of stone supported by five stone legs where farmer's wives used to sell their spare produce to the villagers.

The walk can be extended a short distance to take in Our Lady's Chapel at Mount Grace. The chapel stands on the hillside above Mount Grace Priory and one end is attached to a house. It dates back to the 14th century and may have been used by the Carthusian monks while building Mount Grace Priory. In the 16th century it was a hermitage, the last hermit to live here was Thomas Parkinson, a Franciscan. It is now a place of pilgrimage.

Part of the walk was the Hambleton Drove Road, it leads to the former Chequers Inn, now a farm which serves refreshments. The drove road may have been in use in prehistoric times as a north-south route which avoided the wet lands beside the rivers in the Vale of York. When the lowland roads were turnpiked in the 18th century and tolls were charged this route became popular with the cattle drovers. The drovers would undertake the job of driving herds of up to thousand cattle south from Scotland to be sold in the English markets. There would be regular stopping places beside the road where cattle could be kept overnight — the Chequers Inn was a droving inn.

START: From the market cross in the centre of Osmotherley walk up North End, the road to Swainby. On the outskirts of the village turn left along Rueberry Lane which is part of the Cleveland Way. Eventually the tracks fork, set in the fork is a viewpoint indicator which points the direction to a number of places of interest in the Vale of York stretched out below. The right fork climbs up to the Lady Chapel pleasantly set on the hillside among trees. Return down the same path and continue along the other track passing above Chapel Wood Farm.

The track passes through two gates to reach some mixed

woodland, after passing through the second gate fork right along the path signposted 'Cleveland Way' This path climbs steadily through the trees, at the top continue, keeping the stone wall on your right along the edge of the wood. Pass the communications relay station and 100 yards further on you pass a triangulation pillar on your right, this was the original start of the Lyke Wake Walk. This popular 40-mile walk follows the watershed of the moors to the coast and was devised in 1955 by Bill Cowley.

The track passes through two gates and then follows the broad path across Scarth Wood Moor, ignore the track to the left. The path eventually joins a stone wall and descends into Scarth Nick. While crossing the moor there are excellent views to the north east across the Cleveland Plain. On reaching the road turn right. The unfenced moorland road is part of the Hambleton Drove Road. When the tarmaced road turns right near the car park carry straight ahead and cross a white footbridge. The broad path sweeps up the hillside on the old drove road.

After one and a quarter mile you join the Osmotherley to Hawnby road and bear left. Pass the Chequers Farm, where you may be able to get refreshments, and 50 yards later turn right along a signposted path. Follow a stone wall on your left, at the corner carry straight along the track over the open moor. Pass through a gate and continue descending into Oakdale with a wall on your left.

Turn right near the uninhabited building and pass through a gate and over a bridge, you are back on the Cleveland Way. A lane climbs through a wood and passes along the edge of two fields to reach a road. Turn left, then in 25 yards turn right at a Cleveland Way sign. Walk up the lane for 150 yards, pass the gate to White House then turn left through a stile. Bear right around the farm buildings and the path descends to a footbridge over a stream. Steps lead up through a wood then you cross two fields with Osmotherley church tower in front of you as a guide. Cross over Back Lane and a cobbled path leads suddenly back into the centre of Osmotherley.